SET FREE
through Inner Healing

by Betty Tapscott

Published by
Hunter Books
201 McClellan Road
Kingwood, Texas 77339

Other Books Written By BETTY TAPSCOTT

INNER HEALING THROUGH HEALING OF MEMORIES
THE FRUIT OF THE SPIRIT
OUT OF THE VALLEY
SELF-IMAGE*
PERDONAR Y SANIDAD INTERIOR*
FORGIVENESS AND INNER HEALING*
*Co-Author Father Robert DeGrandis

ISBN 0-917726-24-3

Library of Congress No. 77-94460

ACKNOWLEDGEMENTS

I want to say thank you to Ruthie Rea, my secretary, who typed the original manuscript; to Jackie Garrett who typed and retyped the final copies of the manuscript; to Shirley Stansbery and Sue Birkman who edited the manuscripts; to Bette Jo Cluck who provided a gorgeous "get away" place to begin the book; to Ruby Reppond for her creative help; and especially to my husband, Ed, and family who loved and encouraged me through another book. And finally, to all the ones who allowed their stories to be told, I thank you.*

*All the names in the testimonies have been changed to protect their privacy.

Dedicated to
Tammy
Paul
Steve

CONTENTS

Page

INTRODUCTION

Since *Inner Healing Through Healing Of Memories* was published in 1975, we have received thousands of letters and phone calls from people asking for prayer. Many of the callers were praising the Lord for a healing that had taken place. We praise God for His goodness, mercy, faithfulness, and for His healing power.

Sometimes we have been asked, "Does inner healing really work? Does it last?" I want you to read a letter from a young woman whose testimony is in the earlier book:

> Dear Betty,
>
> I hope you remember me. I will never forget you. You prayed with me on December 20, 1974. I was passing through Houston on my way to _____. Well, I have remained healed and free, and the Lord has given my husband and me a darling baby boy by adoption.
>
> As a result of my inner healing, my husband came to Jesus, and just five

months later, Jesus blessed us with our darling adopted son.

Betty, my life is so different now. How grateful I am to God that He ordered my steps to Houston and sent me to you. How glad I am that you obeyed and took time out of your busy schedule to see me. I wonder what my life would be like now if He hadn't sent me to Houston, but I really don't want to know. All I know is that I'm more free today than I was then.

God bless you very richly, and I look forward eagerly to spending eternity with you . . .

This young woman arrived at our home wearing a black leather jacket, men's jeans, and boots. She had been on a three-month bus trip across the United States. Her plans were to divorce her husband when she returned. "I don't want to be a wife or mother. I hate housework! Besides, I don't love my husband any-more!" she stated emphatically. She was so bowed down from past sins and guilt. But God set her free through inner healing. All the praise and all the glory go to Him.

We have kept in touch with many of the people whose testimonies are in the earlier book. In the last chapter of *Inner Healing* we shared a testimony about a girl who had been a lesbian, chain smoker, and alcoholic. In a drunken stupor, she had run over a child in a foreign country. Guilt became her constant companion after this unfortunate accident. Through inner healing God healed her painful memories and set her free.

She is now in Bible college, and telephones from time to time to let us know what the Lord is doing in her life. Recently, she called to say that she plans to be a missionary. Since her inner healing she is a radiant, dynamic Christian. Such a transformation could happen only through the power of Jesus Christ. She is a new creature. How we thank Him.

I don't want to leave the impression that everyone with whom we have prayed was healed. That isn't so; nor do I want to lead you to believe that everyone keeps his healing. Unfortunately, everyone does not. God is the only one who can heal. He is the greatest psychiatrist, the greatest physician, the only healer. God will do His part, but each person must do his or her part also.

Inner healing is a daily walk, a daily cleansing, a daily forgiving and being forgiven. It is not a "one time experience." It is a process.

We keep our inner healing by turning our backs on Satan, staying in God's Word, praying, praising, staying in a Spirit-filled fellowship, and most important, keeping our eyes on Jesus. We are engaged in spiritual warfare. We don't keep our eyes on Satan with whom we are battling. Even though we may have been set free, if we turn our backs on God, if we take our eyes off Jesus, the evil spirit will return and bring seven other evil spirits with him (Luke 11:24-26). We cannot return to darkness, deceit, and sin, and expect God to allow us to keep our peace of mind and heart.

Dr. Little, in *The Christian and Emotional Problems* says:

> Satan is battling for the minds of men. He can only battle for the Christian's mind when the Christian takes his attention off Jesus Christ and turns back to his self-nature. It is only the Christians who have gone through severe trials and finally have been able to overcome self and keep their eyes on Christ who recognize that their battle was with Satan.
>
> Some counselors urge Christians to use self-control and not to blame Satan for their acts of misconduct. To the self-centered Christian, this too often suggests using more will power in the matter of conduct. The individual turns more and more to self-control. This is exactly what pleases Satan. As long as Satan can bind the individual to self as his object, he can control him.

Praise God! Because of Jesus Christ, we can be set free. God wants us to be whole — spirit, soul, and body. Isaiah 53:5, states, *"... he was wounded and bruised for our sins. He was chastised that we might have peace; he was lashed — and we were healed!"* In this verse, we see the three types of healing: spiritual healing, inner healing, and physical healing. He wants us to be the person He created us to be.

We can be Spirit-filled Christians and in good physical condition, but still be emotional cripples because we are bowed down with inner hurts, negative emotions, and wrong attitudes. In Jeremiah 4:4, the Bible says, *"Cleanse your minds and hearts, not just your bodies..."*

God wants to heal those inner hurts. He wants to heal painful memories. He wants to set us free from the negative habits and emotions that are hindering our Christian walk.

As we shared in *Inner Healing Through Healing of Memories* there are two parts in inner healing: (1) breaking Satan's bondage and reclaiming our inheritance, (2) praying for healing of memories.

The first step in inner healing is reclaiming our inheritance or taking authority over any giants that Satan has sent against you. We can call them giants, evil spirits, chains, or negative forces. It is anything that Satan sends against us to destroy us. Some examples of these giants are fear, resentment, rejection, hatred, anger, depression, suicide, bitterness, selfishness, jealousy, confusion, and unforgiveness. This process of being set free is, in a way, spiritual surgery as God cuts all those growths from us:

> *You were dead in sins, and your sinful desires were not yet cut away. Then he gave you a share in the very life of Christ, for he forgave all your sins, and blotted out the charges proved against you, the list of his commandments which you had not obeyed. He took this*

list of sins and destroyed it by nailing it
to Christ's cross. In this way God took
away Satan's power to accuse you of sin,
and God openly displayed to the whole
world Christ's triumph at the cross
where your sins were all taken away
(Colossians 2:13-15).

The Bible says in Matthew 18:18, *". . . whatever you*
bind on earth is bound in heaven, and whatever you
free on earth is freed in heaven." In James 4:7, God's
Word says, *". . . Resist the devil and he will flee from*
you."

You may say, "Well, I just don't believe in a real
devil." The Bible says in I Peter 5:8, *"Be careful —*
watch out for attacks from Satan, your great enemy.
He prowls around like a hungry, roaring lion, looking
for some victim to tear apart." We are battling the
powers of darkness. But we can be VICTORIOUS. We
can be SET FREE.

God promised us in II Corinthians 3:17, *"The Lord*
is the Spirit who gives them life, and where he is there
is freedom. . ." He tells us in Colossians 1:13,14 that
". . . he has rescued us out of the darkness and gloom
of Satan's kingdom and brought us into the kingdom of
his dear Son, who bought our freedom with his blood
and forgave us all our sins."

There is not one single thing a person can do by
himself to set someone free from Satan; only the
liberating power of Jesus can break the chains of
bondage. God promised us He would break the chains
that bind his people and the whip that scourges them
(See Isaiah 9:4). We have prayed with people and have

actually felt and seen the lifting of oppression as Satan lost his grip.

I want to say that Christians cannot be *possessed*, but they can be *oppressed*. And some churches are filled with oppressed people. Oppression is not reserved by Satan just for the people on the outside of the church. Satan sends trials against each of us; all of us are subject to all kinds of problems: physical problems, financial problems, emotional problems, spiritual problems. But Christians find it especially difficult to accept the fact that Satan sends emotional problems against Christians.

Dr. Quentin Hyder, M.D., in his book, *The Christian's Handbook of Psychiatry* says:

> Many have believed that somehow their newfound relationship with God should necessarily protect them from emotional illness, which is regarded as sin or a punishment for sin . . . . It is not God's executive will that we become sick; but sometimes it is His permissive will. An unsound mind is just as much a sickness as a broken leg or an acute appendicitis. Whereas many Christians can accept a physical illness as being God's permissive will and will seek help from a doctor, they cannot do so with psychological or emotional problems . . . Christians are not exempt, "*. . . for He maketh His sun to rise on the evil and on the good, and sendeth rain on the just and on the*

unjust" (Matthew 5:45 KJV). We are
just as vulnerable to emotional problems
as non-Christians. The difference is that
Christians have additional spiritual re-
sources to rely on, which can help to
lead them out of fear and into power,
love, and a sound mind.

The second step of our inner healing is the healing of
memories. (For a complete prayer for healing of memories, see Chapter VII in the book, *Inner Healing
Through Healing Of Memories.)* This inner healing
process is asking Jesus to walk hand-in-hand back
through every second of your life, healing every hurt.
Since Jesus is the same yesterday, today, and forever
(See Hebrews 13:8), and time and space mean nothing
to Him, He can go back and heal those hurts. Healing
of memories is not digging up garbage; it is throwing
away the garbage that is there.

God told us in Philippians 3:13 to forget the past
and look forward to what lies ahead; but sometimes we
cannot forget the past because there is resentment or
bitterness buried deep down in the wound. Perhaps the
wound is infected with fear or self-pity. God wants to
anesthetize the hurts, to cleanse the wounds, and to
pour the oil of the Holy Spirit into the wound, to heal
us so we can indeed forget the past.

Some people find it hard to believe that God is
interested in everything about them: every thought,
every hurt, every phobia. But the Bible says that He has
every hair on our head numbered (See Matthew 10:30).
He knows when we sit or stand (See Psalm 139:2). He

knows what we are going to say even before we say it (See Psalm 139:4).

Why, then, do we find it so hard to comprehend that He wants to heal every tiny hurt or painful memory, no matter how insignificant the memory might be? Your problem may be only a compulsion or a phobia, but please know that the Lord would have you set free from it.

After ministering in a ladies' meeting in another city, I received this letter in the mail:

> Dear Betty,
>
> I have always loved to eat popcorn. I couldn't pass a popcorn machine without buying a bag. In the evening, I wanted to relax with a big bowl of popcorn. I began to crave popcorn to such an extent, that I suffered from colitis. I knew I had to "kick the habit," but the aroma of popping corn was irresistible, and I'd eat a whole bag, box, or bowl down to the last bite.
>
> At a meeting of Women's Aglow, I listened to you teach about God's healing of memories. I asked God to heal me wherever He saw that I needed it. He saw that I needed healing and deliverance from the craving of popcorn. He took the desire away. I was free to eat or not to eat. He took away the colitis problem, also.
>
> Shortly afterward, the Holy Spirit brought to my remembrance how my

family gathered around a huge dishpan
of popcorn on winter nights in Iowa.
The little pre-schooler in me was return-
ing to the past for fellowship, happiness,
and security, instead of turning to the
Lord of the present. I am praising the
Lord for filling a void in my life . . .

So whatever your problem is, the Lord wants to heal
it.

My friend, Sue Birkman, founder of Challenge
Presents and wife of a Christian psychologist, wrote a
description of inner healing for one of our inner healing
meetings. She described it as follows:

. . . more than a psychological process of
talking out our hurts or a re-education
of old thought patterns. It is the direct
healing power of Jesus Christ which
comes through prayer and heals the
wound of the past. Inner healing is a
process (a journey) that brings us into
deeper love and understanding of God,
others, and ourselves. Through prayer,
we can thank God in all things rather
than dwell on the past. When God satur-
ates a memory, it will never again be
painful.

I couldn't agree more with this explanation.

Another lady wrote:

Your book on inner healing has given me
a new slant about Christ and His healing.
I find it meaningful not only for the

past experiences that need healing, but it
helps me to understand how to put Him
into everyday experiences so that I will
not need a "healing of memories" later.
He will have already been in the experience.

Many people have been healed in group meetings.
Just recently in a group meeting, the Lord revealed to
me that someone was there who had been in a canoe
accident going over some falls. That is pretty specific,
but, praise the Lord, a lady stood up way at the back
of the church; and she came forward to share that she
indeed had suffered a horrible experience when a canoe
capsized going over some rapids. She had been terrified.
Out of about five hundred people, the Lord singled out
this lady to heal that painful memory.

The Lord revealed to Ed in another group inner
healing meeting that someone was there who had
bitterness and hatred even to the point of murder.
After the meeting was over, a lady came up to say that
she had purchased a gun two weeks before. She was
prepared to use it on her ex-husband who was still
threatening to kill her, or she said, "I might even use it
on myself."

Two days later, she came for prayer to be set free
from the oppression she was under. Her problems did
not change immediately, but she felt differently about
them. Her attitude changed even to the point of calling
her ex-husband to say she had forgiven him.

Another lady shared with us what the Lord had done
for her:

. . . at the end of the meeting, as you led us in the healing of memories prayer, something happened to me. As you prayed, I could smell the odor of a hospital so strongly, that it almost took my breath away for just a few seconds. It was so real, that I opened my eyes to see if someone had opened something, but everyone sat still with their eyes closed. The Lord did not bring to mind the memory, but as the next week went by and I read your book, I kept wondering about that smell.

As I came to the prayer in the back of the book, I said, "Lord, as I read this prayer, it is the prayer from the bottom of my heart." Then, I came to the part that said, 'at the moment of birth, if there was a feeling of rejection and unlove . . .' and I couldn't read any more. I started to cry as if I would never stop. I knew I was being released from rejection. I knew I was being healed. And I praised the Lord for it. You know, I have not had that feeling again of being unloved, even when I was not receiving love. That prayer and letting Jesus do the healing has changed me forever.

I also prayed this prayer for my children. If I had caused memories in them

that needed to be healed, I wanted the
Lord to do so.

It is so exciting when the Lord heals, whether He
heals physically or emotionally, whether He heals in a
group meeting or as a person is prayed for individually,
whether He touches him as he reads a book or listens
to a tape, or whether He meets his need as he cries out
to Him all alone. Jesus is the one who heals! Physical
healing and emotional healing are so wonderful, but the
greatest healing and miracle of all is salvation, inviting
Jesus Christ into your heart as your personal Savior.

All healing, whether it is physical, emotional, or
inner healing, I believe, has its foundation in forgiveness: in asking forgiveness of our sins, in accepting
God's forgiveness, in forgiving others, and in forgiving
ourselves. Jesus is our Savior, and we must never lose
sight of Jesus and His shed blood. It is only because of
the fact that He died on the cross for us that we can be
made whole: spirit, soul, and body, and that we can be
a new creation in Him.

Just as there must be a drawing to Him before one
accepts Jesus as his Savior (See John 6:44), so there
must be a total reliance on the Holy Spirit before
praying with someone for inner healing. Words spoken
without the anointing power of the Holy Spirit will fall
on deaf ears.

There is a perfect time for prayer. Always, always,
the person must want prayer and feel a need for
ministry. It does not work for a wife or mother to try
to "trick" a husband or child into coming for help. The
person must be receptive and should come to you for

prayer. If you have to "round up" or "seek out" people to pray with, something is wrong. If the Lord is allowing His healing power to flow through you, it will be so evident that the people will seek you out.

We have prayed with people who have been previously scarred because someone had supposedly received a word from the Lord that he was to pray for them, when in fact, the Lord had not given a word at all; it was just an over-eager person. The Lord does give that word, but we must be certain it is His word and not our idea.

Much damage can be done by overzealous persons who see "demons" in everyone. Some people in seeking a ministry, may do much damage when they pray for others without discernment or word of knowledge, and "cast out" every evil spirit that they feel the other person has.

I'm not giving these guidelines to discourage prayer for inner healing, but only to encourage you to be positive that you are in fellowship with God and are being sensitive to His voice. Then, when He sends someone to you for prayer, you will have the inner knowing, the confirmation in your spirit, that it is of Him. You can rest assured that He will already have prepared their heart. All you need to do is to be obedient and pray, then wait expectantly to see what miracle God is going to perform. Remember to give God all the praise and all the glory.

God is still performing miracles today. We cannot box Him in. His Word says that signs and wonders shall follow them that believe (See Mark 16:17 KJV). His

Word says that in the last days He will pour out His Spirit on all mankind (See Acts 2:17). This is truly what He is doing today. Oh, He loves us so much, and He wants us to be free from all bondage.

Shortly after our first book was written, the Lord placed it on my heart to write another. Almost from the beginning He gave me the title, *Set Free*. From the moment the idea of the book was planted in my mind, I could see the book cover in my mind's eye with butterflies on it representing freedom and life.

Shortly before the cover was to be designed, my daughter, Tammy, was leaving for school one morning and discovered on our front door an absolutely gorgeous butterfly. It was just transfixed on the door. Then, the next day, one of the letters that came in the mail had a commemorative butterfly stamp on the envelope. A butterfly seal was on the back of the envelope. The lady also sent along a butterfly bookmark. To me, it was a love-pat from the Lord and a confirmation of what the cover design was to be. The words Ann had printed on her original bookmark express my sentiments, too:

> For centuries the Christian Church has used the symbol of the butterfly to express the joyous bursting forth of new life from the cocoon of death. The contrast is vivid.
>
> The cocoon is dull, uninteresting, and immobile; but from it comes the butterfly — so intricately beautiful and free.
>
> Not only do we see the victory of Jesus' resurrection in this symbol, but

also the constant reminder that in Him
we too can fly — but our cocoons must
go!

When we shed our old sinful ways, our negative emotions, and when we allow Jesus to break that bondage, we can emerge from our cocoons and be Set Free.

As you read this book, allow the Holy Spirit to speak to you. We have included a prayer at the end of each chapter. Many people have said, "I don't know how to pray. I don't know what to say when I pray." For those who are a little hesitant about praying, we have included a prayer. But, please, YOU talk to the Lord yourself. He is your dearest friend. Talk to Him as freely and openly as you would your best friend.

You are loved, my friend — wherever you are, whoever you are, GOD LOVES YOU! Jesus Christ died on the cross for you. You are a very special person to Him. He wants to help you, to heal you, to lift your burdens, to solve your problems, to mend your broken relationships.

God knows you are hurting, and He does care. He wants to heal your broken heart and bind up your wounds (See Psalm 147:3). He wants to transform you by the renewing of your mind (see Romans 12:2 KJV). He wants to give you a gift: peace of mind and heart (see John 14:27). You don't have to be bowed down in bondage any longer. God wants to set you free.

You   Can   Be

SET FREE.

Chapter 1

SET FREE FROM REJECTION

Do you feel all alone? Do you feel that no one really cares, that no one really understands? Do you feel worthless, inadequate, inferior? Do you feel at times as if you don't have a friend at all? You're not alone. The world is full of lonely, rejected people. We see people many times with smiles pasted on their faces, laughing joyously in a crowd — but way down deep, they are hurting.

Have you ever asked a friend or neighbor, "How are you?" and they quickly and exuberantly answer, "I'm just great, just great, thank you." Then, a few moments later, they realize you really are concerned, that you really do want to know how they are. So they share hesitantly, "No, things are not great; I'm hurting. I have a deep need, and oh! I desperately want someone to pray with me." Then the mask is off, and you are able to agree with them in prayer asking God to cleanse and heal the wound, to set them free from loneliness or rejection.

Let me insert here that I believe in positive confession with all my heart, but God's Word says in Jeremiah 6:14, *"You can't heal a wound by saying it's not there! . . ."* and there are times we need to share with a friend our deep hurts or listen with sensitive ears as they pour out their heartaches to us. Then, through prayer, God can cleanse and heal the wound, and they can honestly say, "Yes, I feel just great," and mean it.

Many Different Reasons for Rejection

There are many different reasons for feelings of rejection. Some people suffer rejection because they were not wanted even from the moment of conception. Perhaps the baby was conceived out of wedlock, during a drunken spree, or during a time when the mother was on drugs, and the thought of having to be responsible for another life was overwhelming and repulsive. Perhaps the mother contemplated or even attempted having an abortion to get rid of that unborn intruder.

We have been told that even before a child is born, if he was unwanted, he will be born with a feeling of rejection. Perhaps this is one reason why a doctor may leave orders for a nurse to give a certain baby "TLC" (tender, loving care). An unwanted child may have physical problems, but he is almost certain to have emotional problems.

I received a long distance phone call one day from another state. A mother asked for prayer for her three-year-old adopted daughter. She explained the child's symptoms: she cried all the time, had deep fears, nightmares, and feelings of rejection. When I asked if the child was there, she replied, "Yes, she's in the other room." I requested that she get her and that she hold the child on her lap while I prayed.

I never once heard the child make a sound, but a few weeks later, I received this letter:

Dear Betty,

Out of desperation I called you to minister to our adopted three-year-old. When we got her, she had been neglected and mistreated by the natural parents. The natural mother had never wanted or accepted her. She would cry and throw such crying fits until I had exhausted my patience and knowledge of what to do. She could keep this up for a long period of time. She would become hoarse and sometimes hysterical. The last one she had, I knew something must be done. She became completely hysterical and kept telling me she loved me.

She was very frightened and didn't want me to leave her. I tried to pray for her, but she would not permit me to, saying things like, "It scares me when you pray."

I had read your book on inner healing and was very impressed by it. I believed this was what Debbie needed, inner healing. She felt rejection because of her natural parents. I called, and you prayed

and ministered to me over the phone.
You told me to hold Debbie on my lap
as you prayed for her.

Debbie is now a changed child. She
has even stopped having those awful
nightmares she used to have night after
night. She is now free from those fits of
crying. Instead of waking up crying in
the morning, she wakes up singing.

Thank God for His ministry of inner
healing that He has raised up . . . .

This child had been unwanted from before birth and
felt rejection even though her adopted parents wanted
her and loved her. She was being bound by a spirit of
rejection that entered before birth and became stronger
when she was mistreated shortly after birth. God said in
Joel 2:25 that He will restore the years that the locusts
have eaten. This is exactly what the Lord did — and He
also broke the chains of rejection and fear that had
kept this child from being able to receive the love her
adopted parents gave her.

Even before we can consciously remember, our mind
records the things that have happened to us. I had
shared on inner healing at a women's meeting in
another state, and the Lord was revealing to me physical problems He was healing. As I shared what the Lord
was saying, a lady stood up and said, "I felt the healing
power of the Lord go through me, but more than a
physical healing, I have received an emotional healing
today from the Lord." And with that, she turned
around and started sharing with the ladies present. She
said:

As Betty was praying the prayer for healing of memories and got to the point at the time of birth, asking Jesus to heal any trauma at that time, I felt a dark oppression lifting. I have always had a void in my life — a dark area. I never knew why, because I was loved by my family. I know Jesus, and have been filled with His Spirit, but there has always been this one dark area I couldn't put my finger on or identify.

I was told by my mother that when I was born, they thought I was dead. I was born prematurely at home. At the time of birth, my mother started hemorrhaging profusely. The doctor had the attending nurse put me in a little shoe box and place me on the table because they thought I was dead.

Then the doctor tried feverishly to save my mother's life. When after a time my mother's bleeding had been stopped and she was out of danger, the doctor took another look at the supposedly dead baby, and to his amazement, he discovered that the baby was alive.

When Betty was asking Jesus to heal all painful memories, I could see Jesus go over to that shoe box, pick up that little premature baby, breathe life into it, and put it on His shoulder, loving and cuddling that tiny baby. At that moment, something on the inside of me was released. I've been healed! I'm free! Praise the Lord, I'm free!

Many times we have listened to adults pour out their hearts, tears running down their faces, sharing, "I can remember my mother saying, 'I didn't want you,' or 'I wasn't ready to quit my job or career, but I became pregnant with you and had to give up my job,' or 'we had all the family we could take care of, then you came along.'"

One grown woman said, "My mother told me she tried to abort me when she found out she was pregnant." The lady involuntarily shivered as she heard her own voice say those words. Another lady said, "My mother left my daddy right after she found out she was pregnant, and she always told me when I was growing up how hard it was to make a living for me. I always felt guilty for her having to work so hard."

One lady said that before she knew she was adopted, if she misbehaved, her mom would say, "I'm going to take you back where you came from." Then, when she was in the fifth grade some thoughtless teacher let slip the information that she was adopted. The girl was shattered. She said, "I kept thinking, Oh, that's what mother meant when she said she was going to take me back — why, she was going to take me back to the orphanage." She lived with her ear "glued" to her parents' door trying to hear if they really planned to take her back or not.

There is a form of rejection that comes from knowing your parents wanted a boy and you were a girl, or they wanted a girl and you were a boy. You felt their disappointment. One lady who had lived her life under the care of different psychiatrists said that her father wanted a boy so badly, and that when she arrived, he deliberately gave her the boy's name he had picked out. When she grew a little older, her daddy would take her along with him out into the fields to be his little helper. She dressed in jeans and boots just like the boy she was supposed to have been. She continued to pour out her heart:

> Then my little sister came along. And oh, she had great big, blue eyes, curly blonde hair and was so beautiful. Dad wasn't disappointed in her being a girl. She was so beautiful, how could he be? They cherished her. But I felt so left out, so rejected, such a misfit, such a disappointment.
>
> My little sister stayed in the house, and did all the woman's work like learning to cook and keep house while I was always out helping Dad with the man's chores.
>
> I wanted to take piano lessons, but they couldn't afford lessons for two girls, so my sister got to take the piano lessons.
>
> I found as I grew older that I really didn't know who I was. I just knew I was miserable and didn't like myself.

With such an unhealthy emotional foundation, is it any wonder that she started seeking love and

acceptance from sources outside her family? Even as a
teenager, she was promiscuous. In marriage after marriage, she sought love and acceptance, always trying to
rebuild a shattered self-image that came when she was
supposed to be a boy and wasn't. In her later years she
began to realize God's love for her. She was finally
beginning to accept herself for who she was, and to
acknowledge that God wanted to heal her.

Another lady shared that she was always introduced
as, "This is Janie*. She was supposed to have been our
boy!" "My little accident" was how another mother
always introduced her little girl, and the words still hurt
her as she repeated them as a grown woman.

Still another mother would say, "This is my change-
of-life baby." Then she would go into detail about how
all the other children were grown, and she was all ready
to enjoy life — "And then Betsy* came along." With
resignation she would continue and say, "Oh, I could
have killed my husband when I found out I was
pregnant."

We hear these same stories over and over. Parents
have no idea what damage they have caused or that
they are causing. But the children have heard these
cruel comments all their lives, and it is like a tape
playing: "I wasn't planned; I really wasn't wanted; I
really was a disappointment." Even though they may
have been loved, cherished, and cared for later on,
those short, one-line phrases such as, "here's my little
accident," or, "this one was supposed to have been a

*Names have been changed

boy," are thought patterns written with indelible ink on their minds.

I want to insert a word of caution (and many of us may have been guilty of this same thing). When a baby is on its way, you may want the child with all your heart. You may be so excited about that little baby. Gradually, the daddy-to-be may say, "I want a boy," or the mother-to-be may say, "I want a girl." You both choose names. You hope and plan, sometimes buying only blue clothes for a boy, or only little pink gowns for the girl on the way.

You know all the time that there isn't one thing that can be done about changing the sex of that child, but you continue to hope for the child of your choice. We must be so careful about getting our heart set on the sex of our unborn child. We have found over and over how damaging the parents' disappointment can be to children if they feel they were the wrong sex. We need to thank God for the baby He is giving us whether it is a boy or girl.

We read in Psalm 139:13-16:

> *You made all the delicate, inner parts of my body, and knit them together in my mother's womb. Thank you for making me so wonderfully complex! It is amazing to think about. Your workmanship is marvelous — and how well I know it. You were there while I was being formed in utter seclusion! You saw me before I was born and scheduled each day of my life before I began to*

breathe. Every day was recorded in your
book!"

I recall the family who had two sons and then many
years later, the wife became pregnant. This baby was
supposed to have been a little girl, but it was another
little boy. This mother has turned that boy into a
clinging, sissy son with effeminate actions and manner-
isms. He is trying to fill the role of the girl that he was
supposed to have been.

Another mother so wanted her sons to be six feet
tall, even though she and her husband were both small.
The sons always knew of her disappointment, not only
in their short height, but also in their sex, because she
had wanted a girl.

The boys were given hormone shots as children by a
doctor to help increase their height. They grew up
feeling rejected and inferior. As the mother shared her
story she cried and said, "Oh, what have I done to my
children?"

Not only did she want her sons to grow taller, but
she kept praying, "Lord, please increase my husband's
height."

I said to her, "Do you realize what you are doing?
You are trying to 'manipulate' God."

She was shocked and said, "I don't know what you
mean."

"You aren't really praying – you are almost demanding that God change the height of your sons and
husband." Then I asked her, "Does your husband love
you?"

"Oh yes, he adores me."

"Does he like you just the way you are?" (And that would have certainly been easy, because she was a beautiful woman.)

"Yes, he loves me just the way I am."

"How would you feel if your husband kept saying, 'Now, I want you to grow two more inches; you're just too short ' or, 'I want you to change the color of your eyes; I always wanted my wife to have blue eyes.' "

"Oh, that would be terrible!"

Then I gently said, "Can you see what you have been doing to your husband and children? They cannot change, and you have been angry toward them and God." I led her into a prayer saying, "God, I ask forgiveness for my resentment and self-will. I forgive You for my husband and my sons being so short. And I thank You for them just the way they are."

It was at that moment when she relinquished their height to the Lord that she started getting relief from the physical problem she was having. She had never realized that not only was she making her sons feel rejected, but her husband as well. Since she has become a Spirit-filled Christian, she is praying that God will heal any hurts she caused her family.

We can and should pray, asking the Lord to make our children spiritually and emotionally what He wants them to be. But we need to thank God for the things we cannot change such as their sex, size, and coloring.

When we think of rejection, we usually think of family circumstances. We can experience that same feeling of rejection in any situation. Are you in a job where you are the only Christian? At lunch time do all the non-Christians deliberately exclude you as they go to lunch? You may feel left out; a little self-pity may creep in, perhaps a little resentment.

It is then that you must say, "All right, God, You have allowed me to be here. I don't like what is happening, I feel left out, but I'm going to praise You and thank You for it. I know You are going to make me stronger because of it." Look around you; there is probably a lonely Christian just like you who is praying, "Please, God, send me a friend." The Bible says in I Thessalonians 5:16-18, *"Always be joyful, always keep on praying no matter what happens, always be thankful, for this is God's will for you who belong to Christ Jesus."*

It's not only in non-Christian families that the feeling of rejection is allowed to enter and grow. Unfortunately, even the pastor's family or the minister's family can feel left out and rejected. Pastors are constantly being bombarded with requests for prayer, and sometimes the family suffers.

When the Lord first led us into this ministry, we were completely overwhelmed with phone calls, letters, and requests. We found ourselves counseling almost every night, Saturday, and Sunday. Then the Lord dealt with us about our own family's needs. It wasn't easy, but we stopped the weekend and the night-time sessions, unless they were an absolute emergency.

There were times when I felt guilty if we were having a quiet evening at home just with the family. I thought, "Oh, there is that long list of people waiting for prayer and counseling." Then I'd remember all the things waiting to be done in the ministry.

I finally had to realize that God gave us our family before leading us into a ministry, and the time Ed and I and the children had together as a family was just as important or more so than anything else. There must be a balance.

What mother has not at times felt a little twinge of rejection as Dad and the children unintentionally gang up on "good old Mom?" Dads, your first responsibility is to your wife. Take up for her; cherish and defend her. If there is a disagreement over disciplining the children, talk about it later, not in front of the children.

There is nothing more damaging than for a father to allow the children to run down their mother. It is so tragic and damaging when one parent subtly or perhaps consciously forms a circle with the children, leaving the other parent out.

There are many situations in which you could feel rejection. Rejection may have come because of the family you were born into or because of the way you were reared (and I want to say here that I thank God for Christian parents who loved me with all their hearts). You may have been rejected by your parents, grandparents, by brothers or sisters, or by stepparents.

Did you have an alcoholic parent? Perhaps you had a parent who was sick all the time and couldn't give you the care you needed. Both of your parents may have had to work, leaving you alone much of the time. If you did not receive love from your earthly father, it may affect the way you feel about your Heavenly Father.

Was your mom always playing bridge or tennis? Was your dad always playing golf or going on hunting trips, and you as a child were left behind? Or as a wife, perhaps even today you're spending much of the time being a "golf" widow. Many wives suffer rejection from having a "workaholic" for a husband.

Natalie's Story*

One girl who never felt her father's love almost ruined her life — until Jesus healed her of her feelings of rejection. Here is her story:

She grew up in a prominent home with a domineering, aggressive father, and a passive mother. She could please neither. Because she felt rejection, she tried desperately to "work" her way into their hearts. She became a facsimile of her father by adopting his aggressive, domineering attitude. However, she tempered these assertive traits by adding a touch of humor and by being concerned with pleasing others. They went to church, more or less, but spiritual values were not that important.

She completed college, became a teacher, and married young. She found herself living with a husband much beneath her social background, one who was brilliant, but with definite neurotic, even paranoid

*Name has been changed

tendencies. She suffered much physical and mental abuse, but could not face failure, so continued to try to make a go of it.

After their son was born, things went from bad to worse; her husband committed adultery. Finally, after narrowly escaping being killed, she divorced her husband, and began again. But nothing seemed to work right. Teaching school became her driving force, and her son, her love.

But still reaching out, she married again — someone six years younger, with none of her traumatic experience. He was passive, and so she became the head of the house, re-enacting her father's role. Very quickly two facts became clear: she did not respect a man whom she could dominate; and worse, as a result of the physical abuse of her first husband, she would become hysterical when having sexual relations with her loving, young husband.

Her marriage was about to break up, when some friends brought her to our inner healing meeting. By now she was desperate enough to "go out and get saved" as she put it. She said the sinner's prayer, and went through the entire group inner healing prayer, and she said, "I felt gloriously free inside." When she got home, she was able that very night for the first time to give and receive sexual love, completely free from all hysterics. The physical side of the marriage became the beautiful, wholesome experience the Lord intended it to be.

The Lord has done so much in her family. Her husband and son became Christians one week later. She has been an administrative intern at a school for a year, and her husband has become the head of their home. They are active in church. Perhaps the best ending to her story is that she's pregnant after refusing to give her husband a child for so many years.

Other Causes of Rejection

Did you grow up feeling you were left out at school, or have you been ridiculed or ostracized at your job? Even in church groups, you may find your close friends turn their backs on you emotionally because they don't understand your new belief in the Lord.

There may even be a time when you feel rejected by your husband, although he loves you with all his heart. Perhaps your children have grown up, and they no longer include you; you feel left out. Old age may find you separated from your friends and family, and you feel lonely and depressed.

Tragically, some people are rejected because of physical reasons: either because of the color of their skin, their unusual looks, or a deformity. The handicapped may suffer from rude stares of the curious. But they may also suffer the cruelty of being ignored and excluded (which for them could be total rejection).

There is a rejection that comes when a friend you trusted turns his back on you. You may not know the reason, you may offer your hand in reconciliation, but he still won't share what the problem is, or be reconciled. Fenelon in *Let Go* says that those who injure us are to be loved and welcomed as the hand of God.

... You must learn to love other people
without expecting any friendship from
them at all. People tend to be quite
fickle. They love us and leave us, they
go and come. They shift from one position to another like a kite in the wind,
or like a feather in the breeze. Let them
do as they will. Just be sure that you see
only God in them. They could do nothing to you without His permission. So,
in the end, it is He that tests or blesses
us, using them as we have need.

You may be hurt because your marriage has ended in
divorce. Has your husband or wife fallen in love with
someone else and wants to marry that one? When you
lose a mate through death or divorce and your world
crumbles around you, Satan will try to devour you with
the giant of rejection.

Sometimes the agony of losing a loved one through
death is easier to cope with and struggle through than
the agony and rejection that comes with divorce. Divorce causes a wound that is constantly being reopened.
Many times there is that sliver of resentment, bitterness,
jealousy, self-pity, or hate way down deep in the
wound that keeps it from healing properly.

You may be suffering the pain of rejection for one
or more of these many reasons, but I want to tell you
that you are never alone. God loves you; He knew
about you before the world began. He allowed you to
be born into your particular family and under those
conditions. If you did not have a happy childhood,

don't dwell on the past, blaming all your heartache and grief on your parents or environment. God tells us to forget the past and look forward to what lies ahead (Philippians 3:13).

If you have any unforgiveness toward your parents, family, husband, wife, children, or anyone else because of rejection, you must forgive them and ask God's forgiveness for your own negative emotions. I know they were not right in rejecting you, but the Bible says, *"Your heavenly Father will forgive you if you forgive those who sin against you; but if you refuse to forgive them, he will not forgive you" (Matthew 6:14,15).*

A Miracle — Spirit, Soul, and Body

The following testimony is of a girl who was completely shattered by the giant of rejection, but her healing is the glorious testimony of God's healing power.

She was beautiful. She had beautiful eyes, beautiful skin, dimples, and a lovely smile. When I told her how pretty she was, in childlike unbelief she asked, "Do you really think so?" She felt so ugly and inferior that she honestly found it hard to believe anyone could think she was beautiful.

Her story was almost unbelievable. There were several brothers and sisters, a quiet, unassuming mother, and a demanding, overbearing father. While the father was away at war, her mother fell in love with someone else and became pregnant. She was born shortly before the husband came home from war.

She said, "You know, I could remember as a child that for really no reason at all, Daddy would hit me or call me in from playing and spank me. Many times I remember playing with my brothers or sisters, and Daddy would jerk a toy from my hands and give it to them."

She continued her tragic story that when she was very young, her father called her in one day with a piece of paper in his hands. He said, "I want to show you this. This is your birth certificate, and you are not mine. You were born while I was away at war." The little girl did not understand all that he was saying, but she certainly understood that she was being told that she was not his, that she was not wanted, that she was not loved as much as the other children.

To add to the already deep, agonizing wound, she was molested repeatedly by her father in her teen-age years. The family obviously was not a Christian one. She said, "Oh, my teen-age years were nothing but a nightmare." She married early to get away from home. She had a baby soon after she married.

Just one year before she came to our house, she accepted Jesus as her personal Savior. She told me, "My life has changed so! There is new meaning and joy." She added that she had even received the baptism of the Holy Spirit.

But then her face clouded, and she said, "Betty, I don't understand. I thought I would change completely. I thought I would be set free from my hatred and bitterness and resentment." Then she added very quietly, "I thought I would be able to show love to my

husband the way a wife should, but I find I am still in
bondage. I still have hatred for my dad. I still feel so
ugly."

She went on to say, "It is breaking my heart because
my husband is not a Christian, and he certainly doesn't
see enough fruit in my life to want to become one."

We prayed for inner healing, asking the Lord to set
her free from all rejection, hatred, bitterness, resentment, inferiority, and the inability to show love. Then
we asked Jesus to walk back through every second of
her life and to heal every painful memory. I kept
reminding her that it was not her daddy who molested
her, but it was the devil working through him.

And then I said something that had to come from
the Lord. I heard myself saying, "You know, you were
conceived in love. From what you said, your mother
detested your daddy, but you were conceived in love."
(Let me hasten to say that I do not approve of
adultery. It is wrong and causes guilt and condemnation.)

Obviously, though, this is what the Lord wanted her
to hear, because her face lit up and she said, "Oh,
that's right. I was born out of love. I was wanted. God
really did know about me." And she added, "God, I
thank You and praise You for allowing me to be born
just the way I was."

The Lord set her free from all those negative forces,
and in His precious way, He very gently cleansed all
those deep wounds. He healed all the painful memories.
A glow came on her face as the Lord's healing power
flowed through her. If she had been beautiful before,

she was absolutely radiant now. She was so filled with
the Spirit, I was actually concerned about her driving
home on the freeway.

As we stood at the door, I said, "You know, I
believe the Lord is saying that when you are able to
give yourself freely to your husband in a wholesome
way, and when he sees the joy of the Lord and God's
healing power working in you, I believe he will come to
Jesus."

She was ecstatic when she called the next morning to
say that her husband recognized the new "her" and
that he instantly saw the transformation in her life.

It was approximately six weeks later that this same
young woman called to say, "Betty, I've just been told
I have a brain tumor, and I must have surgery immediately." I asked her if she could praise God even for
this. She answered, "Yes, I can." And then over the
telephone, we had a beautiful time of praising the Lord
for this valley she was walking through.

We cannot understand God's ways. We cannot see the
complete picture of a puzzle until all the pieces are put
in place. But God says in Ephesians 5:20, *"Always give
thanks for everything to our God and Father in the
name of our Lord Jesus Christ."*

She relied on the Lord. She kept praying and praising
and trusting God even though she didn't understand
what He was doing. It was just before her surgery when
her husband realized that he needed all the inner
strength he could get. He realized how lost he was
without Jesus, and how utterly powerless his life was,
how desperately he needed Him. And in this hour of

need, he cried out to Jesus and accepted Him as his personal Savior.

She went into surgery praising the Lord with complete peace that she was in the Lord's hands. The surgery was successful, and it was just a few days later that I was able to talk to her. She was still rejoicing for all the miracles that the Lord was performing.

She said, "My dad stayed with me almost night and day at the hospital, and he said he just didn't know what he would do if something should happen to me. Betty, he loves me; he really does love me." It reminded me of the scripture in Malachi 4:6, *"His preaching will bring fathers and children together again, to be of one mind and heart. . . ."*

When I called this woman and read the testimony to her to make sure I had all the facts exactly right, she said, "Betty, there are two things I want you to add. Please tell how my feeling of rejection had so adversely affected my physical relationship with my husband."

"Really," she continued, "the only word for it is 'frigidity.' I had been abused and misused so many times, that when my husband approached me with a husband's love, I still felt as if I were being used. But oh, praise God!" she added, "that is all gone. I can love my husband freely now with the love that God ordained. That area of my life has been completely transformed."

She added, "And Betty, my relationship with my dad is completely healed. He is being so thoughtful and loving. He has paid for my wigs since I have lost all my hair, and he spent 200 hours hand-carving something for me. He told my mother it was for his 'dearest little love.' " When I heard that story, I thought, "Oh, thank You, dear Lord, for this miracle of reconciliation!"

Rejection Through Emotional Illness

A mother brought her eight-year-old son and eleven-year-old daughter for prayer one day. The family had suffered much rejection when the children's daddy suffered a nervous breakdown. From a loving, warm husband and father, he became cold and indifferent, lashing out and accusing them for no reason.

This family had a deep, abiding faith in Jesus. It was a delight to see such well-adjusted children, even after going through what they had. The mother was certainly to be commended.

But she explained, "They are getting a little discouraged. They feel some rejection. They have been embarrassed. My son is beginning to have school problems; my daughter doesn't have a good relationship with her teacher this year, and she feels some rejection there. Would you pray with all of us for inner healing?"

We knelt down and took each one separately to the Lord. We took authority in the name of Jesus over the spirits of rejection, embarrassment, frustration, hopelessness, and so on. Then we asked Jesus to heal every painful memory, to fill the void with His love, joy, and peace, and to give them the love of an earthly father that they were missing at that time.

A short time later, the following letter came:

Dear Betty,

Thank you again for praying with us for inner healing. Our son, in telling his brother and sister about it, said it was a "real blessing." On the way home from your house, he said, "You know, we really needed that!" PTL! The day after you prayed, his teacher gave him full credit and released him from completing an assignment she gave him as punishment. He came home walking on a cloud, knowing he was completely forgiven.

Our daughter is back to her usual joyful, pleasant self, knowing she received a touch from God. She is praying for her teacher now and has shared having Jesus stand with you and another person when you're having difficulty with them.

I have experienced a new depth in the peace of God. He has truly wiped away the hurt and healed it completely and then given peace and a return of His joy — not only in how He works, but a joy in Himself.

Rejection From Parent and Husband

Another lady wrote to tell of the healed relationships with her former husband and mother that the Lord brought about after setting her free from rejection. Here is her letter:

My giant was "rejection" — all my life by my mother, followed by a marriage of the same. Finally, through the Lord's guidance in my life, I was given the courage to end my marriage, which had been a series of infidelities, broken promises, and lies. After two separations previously, my ex-husband had even told me he was "saved" in order to get me to return to him; then, after a short while each time, he had returned to his old life of adulteries. So, I had already been through this divorce and was trying to walk in the Christian Way and make a new life for myself.' I truly felt that Jesus was with me in this phase of my day-to-day existence.

I was able to forgive the past. When he came to me two months after the divorce asking for forgiveness and to be reconciled, I said "yes" to forgiving him, but "no" to our getting back together again. So we are friends, and I still pray for his soul; but it has been easy for me to let go and let God work His will in this instance, and I am sure He will accomplish what I was never able to do with all my tears and accusations of the past.

However, the situation with my mother continued to be unresolved. After all, you can't "divorce" your mother. As far back as I could remember, it had been impossible to please her. Neither my sister nor I had been able to live up to her expectations. She did not approve of either of our husbands; in fact, she never did understand why we wanted to get married.

Her marriage with my father had been a disappointment to her, and like my sister and me, my father was never able to please her, either. After his death, she never made any friends of her own age. She did not even attend church regularly.

Needless to say, our family was in a state of constant bickering all these years, quarreling over what we should do about our marriages, our children, our homes, etc., with her constantly being the "martyr" whom nobody loved or appreciated. My sister and I alternated between feeling guilty, trying to do things to please her, and being very hateful and argumentative with her. We always felt rejection.

My sister developed a disease which left me as my mother's only source of help in running errands for her and driving her to various places. Therefore, she had become more and more of a burden upon me, particularly with my marriage situation and a very demanding job. I had reached the point where just to hear her voice on the phone complaining or demanding was enough to cause me to "come unglued."

Even though she lived near me, she continued to keep her bank account at a bank across town in her old neighborhood. She said she did not intend to put her bank account in a bank near us as "it didn't hurt us to do these things for her." If we bought groceries or clothing for her, she never liked the brand or the color.

She always felt you could get things cheaper if you went to the discount stores which are across town. If she needed medicine, it should be purchased at a store other than the neighborhood drug store. I had become so resentful; and even though I would go ahead and do things her way, I would quarrel with her about it and then feel guilty afterward.

This was the situation when I got in your prayer line that morning at the seminar. You paused in front of me with your sweet smile and understanding eyes.

I had been on my knees in the back of the room when you prayed your general prayer for inner healing, and tears of remorse and guilt had filled my eyes about this situation.

When I explained it all to you briefly, you said to do all these things for Jesus, not my mother. Of course, you said more than that, but that was the general message. Betty, except for two or three times since then, for which I have begged my Lord's forgiveness, I have put your instructions into practice, and they have worked.

First of all, I do not believe that Jesus would expect me to do unreasonable things which require all my extra time and strength. Therefore, I have begun to do things for her in the same manner in which I run my own business, which actually is an efficient and time-saving operation.

Quietly, without any argument, I moved Mother's bank account to where I bank, so the drive-in window is within minutes of her house rather than an hour away. I do her shopping at stores closer by. The time I have saved, not to mention the gasoline, has been a bonus I have used to be more involved in my church activities, visit relatives and friends, and just spend time alone with my Lord and reading.

More remarkable has been my mother's attitude. She seems to have completely accepted the fact that things are being done differently, and even though she still complains about certain things, when I don't argue or quarrel with her, she soon forgets it.

We have truly enjoyed being together on a few evenings lately when I have taken her out to dinner or visited with her. When she starts to complain or becomes argumentative, I simply pray instead of answering her back. I've also given her some of the books I've been reading, and even though she says she hasn't read them yet, I wonder. Somehow, she seems to be changing a lot also. Praise the Lord!

Smile, God Loves You

A lady who came to our house for prayer said, "I'm a Spirit-filled Christian, but I feel so worthless, inadequate, and inferior. I can't do anything for the Lord."

I said, "Oh, yes you can! You can witness to every person you come in contact with."

She shared that she had always felt a sense of rejection and believed herself to be ugly. Actually, she was a lovely, tall, and attractive woman, but she felt big and ungainly. She said, "My sister was tiny, and it seemed she could always do everything right."

As she talked, I began to notice something. She never smiled; *never!* I thought, "I believe if this lady smiled, her face would crack."

She said, "I'm sure my mother loved me, but she was always finding fault with everything I did. I felt I could never do anything right. I have always felt rejection and failure."

We prayed, asking the Lord to set her free from the spirits of rejection, inadequacy, unworthiness, jealousy, and fear of failure. Then we asked Jesus to heal every painful memory, to fill the void with His love, joy, and peace, to fill her to overflowing with all the fruit of the Spirit.

It seemed the Lord was saying to me, "I want you to teach her how to smile." So, I asked, "Will you do something for me? Will you push up right here on either side of your cheeks with your hands and smile?" This seemed almost ridiculous, but bless her heart, she did as she was asked to do. As she pushed up on her cheeks, she began to smile. And, you know, her face didn't break! Real joy welled up from down deep inside her and began to bubble forth.

I said, "I want you to share God's love and peace to everyone you come in contact with at work. Remember, we don't 'go' witness. We 'are' a witness every moment of the day to everyone we meet." She was a payroll clerk, so she saw all the employees twice a month. "On the next payday as each person comes for his check, I want you to give him a great big smile and silently pray in the Spirit for him, asking God to bless and help him to use his money wisely." She left rejoicing in the Lord. She felt peace and contentment and was smiling from ear to ear.

In about two weeks, the phone rang at 5:30 in the afternoon. It was this same lady, just praising the Lord. She said, "Let me tell you what has happened. I've been doing as you told me to. And today was payday. I gave everyone a great, big 'Jesus smile,' praying for each one as I gave him his check. Apparently, there was a change in me, because three people turned around and said, 'Hey, what has happened to you? You're so different!' "

The Bible says when we are in Christ old things are passed away; all things become as new and we are new creatures (see II Corinthians 5:17 KJV). She indeed was a new creature in Him. By applying God's principle in Romans 12:2 KJV, *"Be ye transformed by the renewing of your mind,"* she was able to forget the past life of rejection. She now knew she was a child of the King, a joint-heir with Jesus, a very special person with a special job to do. Her office and pay-roll position was her point of contact to witness for Jesus.

Have you felt rejection? Do you feel rejection now? Let me say again, He knew about you before the world began. God loves you. He cares for you. You are so special to Him. Jesus would have died on the cross for you if you had been the only person on this earth. You are so precious to Him. You are the apple of His eye. He wants to be all things to you, your father, your family, your friend, your advocate, your defender, your

provider, your shield. He wants to meet your every
need. God wants to set you free from the giant of
rejection and the fear of rejection. He wants to heal
your painful memories. He wants to fill the void with
His divine love. Remember, your Heavenly Father loves
You — very, very much.

You are loved, My Friend!

PRAYER FOR REJECTION

Father, I come to You in the name of Jesus. Thank
You for giving me life and for loving me. I bind the evil
one from me in the mighty name of Jesus. Spirits of
rejection and fear of rejection, you are bound and cast
out in the name of Jesus. Spirits of loneliness, self-pity,
and inferiority, you are bound in the name of Jesus.

Jesus, please go back into the third and fourth
generations and break all harmful, genetic ties. I know
You were there from the moment of conception. If any
negative force came against me before I was born, I
pray that You will go back even to that time and set
me free and heal me.

Please, Jesus, fill me with Your love. I pray that You
fill the void and give me all the love I needed as a child
but did not receive. I forgive anyone who did not give
me love. I forgive my parents if they did not always
show me love; I forgive my brothers or sisters if I was
compared to them or if they did not give me love. I
forgive my mate or children if they did not show me
love.

Thank You, Jesus, for going back through every
second of my life, for being there every time I felt

unwanted, rejected, or lonely. Thank You for cleansing all the wounds, and binding up my broken heart. Please fill me with Your precious love to overflowing so I can love those around me. Please fill me with the fruit of the Spirit. It's in Your name, Jesus, that I pray. Amen.

Scriptures on Rejection

Psalm 139:13-16 "You made all the delicate, inner parts of my body, and knit them together in my mother's womb. Thank you for making me so wonderfully complex! It is amazing to think about. Your workmanship is marvelous — and how well I know it. You were there while I was being formed in utter seclusion! You saw me before I was born and scheduled each day of my life before I began to breathe. Every day was recorded in Your Book!"

I Peter 1:2 "Dear friends, God the Father chose you long ago and knew you would become his children. And the Holy Spirit has been at work in your hearts, cleansing you with the blood of Jesus Christ and making you to please Him. May God bless you richly and grant you increasing freedom from all anxiety and fear."

Psalm 68:5,6 "He is a father to the fatherless; he gives justice to the widows, for he is holy. He gives families to the lonely . . ."

Psalm 139:17,18 "How precious it is Lord, to realize that you are thinking about me constantly! I can't even count how many times a day your thoughts turn towards me. And when I waken in the morning, you are still thinking about me!"

Chapter Two

SET FREE FROM FEAR

Fear is an emotion that has come against every person some time or another. Fear can be a most crippling, devastating emotion; fear breeds fear. Satan builds on fear until some victims even have a fear of being afraid, and they live in a vicious cycle of fear.

Fear has been with us since Adam and Eve. In fact, theirs was the first recorded fear. Genesis 3:10 KJV says, *"... I heard thy voice in the garden, and I was afraid ..."*

Name any activity, and someone, somewhere, probably has had a fear concerning it. Here is a limited list of some of the fears people have:

Acrophobia .... Fear of heights
Agoraphobia .... Fear of going outside the home
Ailurophobia .... Fear of cats
Androphobia .... Fear of men
Arachnephobia .... Fear of spiders
Astrephobia .... Fear of thunderstorms
Autophobia .... Fear of being alone

Carophobia . . . . .Fear of insects
Claustrophobia . . . . .Fear of enclosed places
Demophobia . . . . Fear of crowds
Gamophobia . . . . Fear of marriage
Gynephobia . . . . Fear of women
Hemophobia . . . . .Fear of the sight of blood
Laliophobia . . . . .Fear of speaking in public
Lyssophobia . . . . .Fear of going insane
Necrophobia . . . . Fear of dead bodies
Nyctophobia . . . . Fear of night or darkness
Pyrophobia . . . . .Fear of fire
Scopophobia . . . . Fear of being observed
Zoophobia . . . . Fear of animals

Surely, each person can remember occasions when he felt some type of fear. For a second, your heart pounded, your throat became dry, you felt "butterflies" in your stomach. When fear causes a person to limit an activity or to refrain from doing a certain thing, then we must realize that Satan is in control, and the fear has ceased to be harmless and has become an obsession or a phobia.

Fear can become like heavy chains around us. But praise the Lord, Isaiah 9:4 says, *"God will break the chains that bind his people and the whip that sourges them . . ."*

Fear comes against the rich and poor alike. Fear knows no age limits; it comes against all people — from birth (perhaps with the fear of choking) to old age with the fear of dying.

A sudden clap of thunder may make a baby scream in terror. A strange face peering over the crib to grin and "coo" at the newborn can frighten a child and send him into hysterics until he is picked up, loved, and cuddled by his mother or daddy.

Fears from School Situations

Going to school, for some children, brings on new fears: fear of the teacher, the principal, fear of getting on the wrong bus, or of being lost. The fear of speaking in front of a group sometimes comes from a simple classroom situation, but one that was embarrassing and humiliating. The following testimony is an example:

When I heard the doorbell ring one morning, I had expected to see the lady who had an appointment for prayer for inner healing. So, I was surprised when I opened the door and saw someone else standing there. It was a friend who explained that she was to drive the other lady over, but when that lady couldn't come, she decided to come in her place.

After we had exchanged pleasantries, she said, "Betty, I don't know if I need inner healing or not, but there is one tiny area in my life that keeps bothering me. I'm so afraid to stand up in front of a group to speak. I'm so embarrassed. My husband and I have just been asked to teach a large group at church, and the thought terrifies me. I know this fear is from Satan; I know I can be set free, and I want to be."

I said, "Let me ask you some questions, and let's see if we can find out when this fear entered. Did you have a happy childhood?"

"Oh, yes," she said, "I was loved and cherished."

"Did you have an early encounter with Jesus as your personal Savior?"

"I surely did," she replied. "In fact, I grew up in the church and accepted Jesus at a very early age."

"Did you ever have any big, traumatic experience — either an accident or illness?"

"No, I didn't. I had a very happy, normal, safe, loving childhood."

I knew this friend as a dedicated, Spirit-filled person who loved the Lord with all her heart. She and her family had experienced a miracle in their family when their little girl was healed from CF. They had walked by faith, standing on God's promises.

The answer to the question, "When did this fear enter?" was not evident. The Holy Spirit would have to reveal to us when this fear entered. We knelt before the Lord and prayed, asking the Holy Spirit to reveal what episode had caused this fear. Soon it was revealed that something happened in the third grade. I stopped praying and asked her to think back to the third grade. Quickly, she said, "Oh, I know what it was." This was her story:

> It was the first day of school. I was so shy, so afraid, so withdrawn. The little boy behind me dropped his ruler on the floor. It made a loud, clattering sound. The teacher responded with a finger pointed right at me and said, "You pick up that ruler right now!"
>
> I very quietly said, "It's not mine. I didn't drop it."

Then with frustration and anger, the teacher came back to my desk and shouted, "I said, pick up that ruler!" So, with fear and trembling, I bent down and picked up the ruler and handed it to her.

She quickly said, "Put out your hand." As I placed my hands before her, she vigorously slapped my hands and knuckles with the offending ruler.

As if that were not enough, she added, "Now, you go out in the hall." Every eye in the room was on me. I felt such fear, embarrassment, anger, (which I was afraid to express), and such guilt. I walked quickly out of the room thinking I was escaping all the eyes on me — when who should walk by but the principal. He wanted to know what had happened, and I tried to explain.

Oh, the embarrassment! I felt such condemnation. And you know, from that time on, getting up in front of a group was agony. In high school and in college during speech classes (taken trying to compensate and overcome this fear), when I was to give a speech, my heart would pound, my hands would become clammy, my arms felt as if they had water in them, my stomach became queasy. I felt as if I had a lump in my

throat. My mouth would become so dry
— oh, it was horrible.

I explained, "Do you see what Satan has done to you? For some reason, you had a weakness to begin with — a shyness. When Satan worked through your distraught third-grade teacher, and she punished you unjustly, this added another layer on the onion of fear. Each additional added episode of getting up before a group proved to be another layer of fear and embarrassment."

"What the Lord does is to go to the core of the onion, so to speak, to remove the root cause of your problems."

I continued, "You know I can do nothing to heal you, but let's invite Jesus back into that childhood experience that was so painful, and ask Him to walk through that experience with you."

"Now picture Jesus; He is in that classroom with you. As the teacher hears the ruler drop and as she comes over to get you to pick up the ruler, picture Jesus bending down and picking up that ruler for you. When the teacher said, 'Put out your hands,' what do you think Jesus would have done if He had been there?"

"Oh!" she said with excitement, "He would have taken the slap on the knuckles for me — just the way He took the stripes and died on the cross for our sins." And in that precious moment, Jesus proved He was the same yesterday, today, and forever (See Hebrews 13:8), and He healed that painful memory.

As she stood at the door to leave after we had finished praying, I felt led to pray one last prayer: "Lord, give her a chance to know she has been completely set free from the fear of speaking in public."

God is so faithful. Within two months, a group of ladies was invited to go to a country in Central America to share Jesus Christ. My friend was one of the twelve invited. And praise God, as she stood before a group of two hundred ladies and shared her testimony and love for Jesus, completely free of fear or embarrassment, I thought my heart would burst with gratitude to our heavenly Father for setting her free and healing her.

Have you ever had stage fright? You were afraid of standing up in front of people and forgetting your answers or lines, of having your mind just go blank. How many of you remember the agonizing fear before a piano or voice recital? Your hands were clammy, your knees weak, there were many trips to the bathroom.

If you have a fear of speaking in public or before groups, remember the Bible says in Mark 13:11 KJV, *". . . take no thought beforehand what ye shall speak, neither do ye premeditate: but whatsoever shall be given you in that hour, that speak ye: for it is not ye that speak, but the Holy Ghost."* This is not to imply that we are not to study to show ourselves approved — of course we are to prepare, and to pray. What He is promising us is that He will be with us when we stand in front of a group of people to speak. If you have a fear of speaking in public, would you pray this prayer:

PRAYER FOR FEAR OF SPEAKING IN PUBLIC

Dear Lord, I ask that You set me free from this fear of speaking in public. Spirit of fear, you are bound and cast from me in the name of Jesus.

Please, Lord Jesus, go back to the very first time I was embarrassed or felt fear before a group. When I forgot my lines in a school play, or I forgot my piano piece at a recital, or when I was embarrassed by a teacher or by class- mates — at school or Sunday School, please take a spiritual eraser and wipe away those memories.

Lord Jesus, I pray that You will fill me with Your power, Your love, and give me a sound mind. Thank You for giving me the confidence and boldness that I need. I will give all the praise and glory to you, Lord Jesus. It is in Your name I pray. Amen.

Fear of Dentists or Doctors

Who hasn't, as a child, suffered fear as he sat down in the dentist's chair and saw for the first time all the strange-looking instruments? Fear of dentists is not just limited to children. A precious friend from another country, a very intelligent person, had such an overpowering fear of dentists, that she asked me to meet her at the dentist's office and pray for her before her appointment.

We agreed to do this and arrived about thirty minutes early. The time was spent reading the Bible, praying, binding the spirit of fear in the name of Jesus, and asking Jesus to fill her with His perfect love. She realized as a new Spirit-filled Christian that God could set her free from this fear — and He did!

When it came time for her appointment, she walked happily into the office with her Bible tucked under her arm. In just a few minutes, she came back out of the office just bubbling and grinning from ear to ear. She said with her beautiful accent, "Oh, praise the Lord! I was not afraid one tiny bit!" This just proves that when we resist the devil, he will flee (see James 4:7).

As parents we should try to explain to our children what the dentist, doctor, or nurse will be doing. It's not so much the fear of the pain, as it is fear of the unknown that bothers children.

We encourage that fear when we aren't honest with them. Our shallow responses of "Oh! It's not going to hurt one bit," come ringing back in their ears when they do have to get an injection; etc., and they find out, "Hey! That needle does hurt!"

It's so much better to explain what will take place, step by step. It instills trust in us when we say, "Yes, the needle will sting just for a moment, then it will be over;" or "Yes, I know you are frightened, but we are right here with you," or "the surgery will hurt, but you will feel so much better in a few days."

Today most doctors, nurses, and dentists do such a beautiful job of explaining to children about the instruments and what the treatment consists of. However, occasionally traumatic experiences do occur. Our oldest son was facing eye surgery when he was four years old. The morning of the surgery, a new nurse came to give him is pre-operative injection.

There he stood, four years old, frightened; and in the doorway stood a nurse with the biggest looking needle I have ever seen. She said, "See what I have for you?" I was appalled that a nurse could be so thoughtless. He was standing by the bathroom door, and he closed the door, pushing in the lock button on the knob. It took about fifteen minutes to be able to get him out of the dark locked bathroom to take the injection she had for him.

Fortunately, he had no painful memories of that experience or of the long days of having both eyes bandaged. But, it was only God's grace and the answer to many prayers that this trauma did not scar him emotionally.

I prayed for a nurse anesthetist one day for inner healing. When we finished I also felt led to pray that God would anoint her face and her eyes with a supernatural manifestation of his love and compassion. I've wondered many times about the people to whom she administered anesthesia, whether they felt added comfort and peace because the love of Jesus was on her face and in her eyes.

Fears of Cats and Insects

Many children are frightened by cats, dogs, water, heights, needles, the dark, storms, elevators, etc. The fears may follow them into adulthood. As adults, they try to overcome their fears, and feel embarrassed because of their hang-ups. They try to use their intellect and reason the fears away, but the fears remain like heavy chains weighting them down.

We prayed with a lady from Holland who had many fears, especially the fear of cats. She had mentioned on the way to our home, "I hope they don't have cats." And what do you think greeted her at our front door? One of our cats! After prayer for inner healing, and she was getting ready to leave that night, our affectionate Siamese cat walked into the living room. I said to the lady, "Now is the time to check and see if your fear is gone." She hesitantly bent down and petted her. Praise God. When she returned to Holland we received a letter from her stating:

> "My fear for cats has changed. My friend
> has such a nice, new cat that I have
> stroked her."

A lady in Canada had such an overpowering fear of caterpillars that she was afraid to go into the garden. When we prayed for this fear I had her picture Jesus holding a caterpillar in His hand. (Personally, I think our Creator had to have a sense of humor to make a fuzzy caterpillar.)

I asked her to picture Jesus talking to her about the insect He had made. She was a delightful person and with all honesty she said, "I can *picture* Jesus holding the caterpillar. I can *look* at the caterpillar, but I don't think I can *hold* it, even in my imagination." We bound the spirit of fear in the name of Jesus and asked Him to heal her.

When we were back ministering in the same city four months later, we saw this lady again. She shared that the Lord had indeed taken her fear away and that she had been able to go out into the garden all summer — free from fear of the woolly little caterpillar.

She had also been healed of excruciating pain in her fingers and hands. The pain had been so severe she couldn't sew. Even to move the car seat had been agony. But praise God! He made her whole: in spirit, soul, and body.

Fear of Heights

A lady wrote that the Lord had healed her of a fear of heights which she acquired when she was just a little girl. Here is her testimony:

> When I was approximately seven or eight years old, our class went on a field trip to a coal mine. In order to reach the entrance, there were a couple of flights of stairs to go up. I was on the outside next to the railing, and the stairs were packed like sardines with kids pushing and shoving.

> As I looked over the railing, visions of me lying on the floor below totally crippled my mind, and fear swept through my entire body. In desperation, I planted myself on the stairs, sitting with my face buried in my hands so I couldn't see the pushing or look over the

railing. I sat there crying and refusing to move. Some man was kind enough to pick me up and carry me to the top of the stairs.

From that day on, the fear of heights was implanted in my mind. The fear became so over-powering in the years that followed, that when I was in tall buildings, I couldn't even go to the windows to look out.

In June of 1976, I went on a Christian cruise sponsored by Charles and Frances Hunter. With them on the cruise were Ed and Betty Tapscott. I remember that while on the cruise, my mother kept leaning against the rail to look at the scenery. There I would always be, pulling on her arm, telling her to get away from the side.

I kept reminding her that she might fall into the ocean. The first couple of days on the ship I never got close to the rail. There was always that HUGE possibility that I would fall overboard. I could just hear the shouts in my mind from people on the ship, "Somebody is overboard!" and there I would be floating in the ocean. With those thoughts in mind, I always made sure I stayed clear of the railing.

While on the cruise, Betty Tapscott led a prayer for inner healing. During the entire prayer, my mind was fixed on my sister, and I didn't realize that Jesus was dealing with fears that were locked up in my sub-conscious.

After the meeting with the Tapscotts, my mother and I went out on the deck. As we were walking around and talking about Betty's prayer, we stopped to admire the scenery. To my surprise, I found myself leaning against the railing, taking in the beauty of the ocean.

Suddenly, it occurred to me that Jesus had healed me of my fear of heights. It was a simple and painless removal which could only have been performed by the Great Physician. A fear that controlled me for years was removed in just a few minutes. Now, when in high places, I am able to enjoy the beauty of God's creation. Blessed be His holy name!

Scary Movies, Goblins and Witches

A young man whose fears led to a nervous breakdown, was under the care of a psychiatrist when he came to us for prayer for inner healing. The Holy Spirit revealed that the fears entered when he was just a little boy and had gone to horror movies every Saturday morning. He said, "You know, I remember leaving the theater literally shaking because I was so afraid. When I started to school, I was so filled with fear." Fear played such a big part in his life that it almost overwhelmed him. He was afraid to leave home or be alone, even as a grown young man. But praise the Lord he has been healed by the power of Jesus.

How many children are frightened by "goblins and witches" on Halloween night, (a supposedly safe, children's fun night)? We stopped celebrating Halloween at our home. Surely, we as Christians have better things to do than to allow our children to go dressed up in devil and witch costumes, scaring one another.

Let's not compromise with the devil. It may be fun and games to us, but it certainly is not to him. Besides the spiritual and emotional damage, it is not physically safe. (Just read the headlines after each Halloween night of the children poisoned, molested, or injured.)

I think it is appalling for Christian churches to show horror movies to their young people on Halloween night. We must not pollute our minds or allow our children to suffer from mind-pollution.

I certainly don't mean to place so much emphasis on fear that we become afraid that we're going to become afraid. Nor do I want us to constantly point fingers at the thing or person who caused the fear.

But we need to look honestly at our fears, walk toward them, take authority over them in the name of Jesus and know with all confidence that we can be set free from fear. Jesus came that we might have life and have it more abundantly (see John 10:10 KJV).

Fear of Driving

Many times fears have no reason. There are many different types of fears. What may be terrifying to one person would not bother someone else at all.

When we first moved to Houston, I had a fear of driving on the freeway. And if you live in Houston, you have to get on the freeway to get to most places quickly. But praise God! He set me free from this fear. I knew I had been set free when I was coming back from the medical center after visiting someone in the hospital.

It was 4:30 in the afternoon, in bumper-to-bumper traffic; and it was raining so heavily, you could barely see in front of you. I fastened my seat belt, and praised the Lord for His guardian angels stationed around the car. All seventeen miles home I sang in the Spirit, completely free from all fear.

A note to remember: Don't expect Satan to give up easily. He will try to keep on harassing you. We must still keep on our armor. Even though I've been delivered from that fear, each time I start to drive, I bind Satan in the name of Jesus and ask the Lord to station His guardian angels around me.

I whisper a prayer something like this, "Lord Jesus, I know You are with me wherever I go; that includes this freeway. Thank You for making my mind and eyesight alert. Thank You for keeping me safe." I pray in the Spirit most of the time when I am driving. It is a wonderful time to pray and praise God.

Set Free From Agoraphobia

Fears do not have to be life-threatening to be damaging. Consider the fear of failure. If you were never praised as a child, if everything you said or did was scrutinized and "picked to pieces" by your parents or older brothers or sisters, the fear of stating an opinion or of making a decision may follow you into adult life. If you were always called names like clumsy, stupid, dumb, crazy, nutty, etc., you may have such a poor self-image that you are afraid to attempt to do anything. You may be afraid to go into new situations or meet new people or even enter into a conversation.

Many children grow up with the fear of being rejected, because they did not receive love as a child. Some women have a fear of men in their adult lives because they were molested as children or did not receive love from their fathers. Lack of an earthly father's love can even cause women and men alike to be afraid of God.

The following is the story of a lady who had been so tortured and mistreated as a child that she was an emotional cripple. She was so afraid of people and of leaving her home; but the Lord performed a miracle and made her whole.

The Lord allowed my eyes to be drawn to her face during a meeting in Canada. Even out of six hundred people, He pointed her out. You could see the lines of fear, agitation, near panic written on her face. After the meeting, someone brought her to me for prayer. Her story was almost unbelievable.

She had been beaten and tortured as a child, and in some ways, treated worse than an animal. Some of her teeth had been knocked out. She had been ostracized, punished, threatened, and always unloved. This little girl did survive and grow up, but she grew up to be an emotional cripple, an agoraphobic. She was completely filled with fear, especially the fear of going outside her home.

She was married, and even had children, but she had to have a member of her family with her every moment. Going outside the home was agony for her. The day before the meeting, she had stayed in bed with the covers pulled up around her chin, just terrified of life.

But praise God! He is the God of the impossible, and He did the impossible that night. He set her free from fear. The Bible says, ". . . *if the Son sets you free, you will indeed be free" (John 8:36)*. The Lord cut those chains of fear that had been binding her.

After we had finished praying for inner healing, I said, "Now, in the morning, I want you to do something you haven't been able to do before. Walk out of the house trusting and believing that the Lord has indeed set you free."

The next night at the meeting in another church, the Lord again allowed my eyes to be drawn to her face. But her face was no longer filled with fear and terror; it was glowing with the love of Jesus.

She shared what the Lord had done for her. "I did walk out of my house this morning without my coat or purse. I walked to the bottom of the hill completely free from all fear. I saw my friend, and I told her what had happened — that God had healed me. My friend asked, 'Can I go to that meeting with you tonight'?"

The friend arrived late, and there were no more available seats, so she had to stand the entire time. During the prayer for salvation for those who would like to invite Jesus into their hearts, the friend accepted Jesus.

Then the Lord gave me a word of knowledge that someone was being healed of an excruciating headache; it was that little friend standing way in the back whom the Lord had healed.

Then the Lord gave me a word of knowledge that someone had just been set free from hatred and unfor- giveness toward her husband. Praise the Lord — it was the same little friend! She was going home to forgive her husband. She was healed spiritually, physically, and emotionally. Isn't God good?

All this took place because the first lady shared that the Lord had set her free and healed her of her fears.

When we returned to Canada four months later, the church staff said that she had been sharing her testi- mony everywhere about what the Lord had done for her. In fact, we had her stand in front of the entire church and tell about being set free from fear. In four months, she had witnessed to six people who had this same fear, and as she prayed for them, they, too, had been set free from fear. Praise the Lord!

God does not heal us just for ourselves, but so that He might be glorified. He wants us to share with others what He has done, and He wants us to give Him all the credit and all the glory.

Fear of People

Most fears are learned or instilled in us. How I shudder to hear a mother or daddy or someone else saying to a child, "If you don't behave, a policeman is going to get you." Consequently, from a very early age the child will consider a policeman someone to be feared instead of a friend and protector. Mothers sometimes instill a fear of the child's father by saying, "Boy, just wait until your daddy gets home. He's going to let you have it." Without realizing it, the mother has planted a seed of fear in her child's mind.

Fear of certain races of people runs rampant in some families. The Lord has a sense of humor and really does know what is best for us. Recently, three boys from Canada came for prayer for inner healing. One of the boys had a deep fear of black people. He had really been terrified to come to the southern part of the United States, and Houston in particular.

When we took them to the rehabilitation center where they were to stay for two nights, who should meet them at the door but a great big, tall, young, black man just beaming with the love of Jesus all over his face. In fact, it was this radiant black Christian who offered the three boys a place to sleep. The Lord allowed these boys and this black man to be roommates in order to tear down the boy's prejudice and fear of a certain race of people. Hallelujah!

As we said earlier, most fears are not life-threatening fears, but they can become so emotionally crippling, that the person cannot function as a normal human being. However, doctors have said that fear and anger both can bring on heart attacks.

Not all fear is bad. There is that terrifying fear or moment of panic that comes when our life or our child's life is endangered, that moment of sheer terror when we see our child step off the curb into the path of an approaching truck, or when we see a huge wave sweeping him out into the ocean. In that moment, our adrenalin starts flowing in our bodies in such a way that we can act more quickly, run faster, or have additional strength to rescue our child. Except in times such as these when God has given us that extra awareness and strength, fear is from Satan. II Timothy 1:7 KJV says, "... *For God hath not given us the spirit of fear; but of power, and of love, and of a sound mind.*"

Many times we don't want to be completely honest concerning our fears. We try to reason them away. We may try to hide the fact that we have a fear from our friends or family. But in Jeremiah 6:14, the Bible says, *"You can't heal a wound by saying it's not there!"*

So let's look at our fears. Admit, "Yes, I have allowed this fear to come against me, but because of the shed blood of Jesus, I can be set free." Remember, you can bind the spirit of fear in the name of Jesus. You can be set free.

You don't even have to have someone pray with you. It is the healing power of the Lord that sets us free.

A lady wrote:

> A copy of your book *Inner Healing Through Healing of Memories* was recently given to me, and Praise the Lord, as I read it and prayed the prayers I soon discovered that I've been relieved

of fears of cats and water, as well as
memories of my mother's death through
cancer, and my father's murder.

Thank you, Lord, for healing this lady. It is through
His Spirit that we are set free and healed.

Fear of the Telephone

One of the most unusual fears we have heard of was
the fear of a telephone. My husband and I were on a
Christian cruise when a school teacher asked us to pray
for the fear she felt when she heard a telephone ring.

After she said, "My stomach gets in knots when the
phone rings," I thought that surely she must have
answered the phone once when there had been a death
message or a message of a terrible accident. She said,
"No, nothing like that ever happened. In fact, I have no
idea where this fear came from."

Praise the Lord that we do not have to know. Our
Heavenly Father knows. At the Holy Spirit's leading, I
asked her to picture Jesus calling her on the telephone.
I felt a little foolish asking a dignified school teacher to
do something so childish.

But she agreed. "I want you to imagine the phone
ringing," and even at that moment, just as the
imaginary phone rang, her body stiffened. In her mind's
eye she started to walk across the room and answer the
phone. All this time I kept saying, "Remember, Jesus is
calling you on the phone. He is there and He loves
you."

As she picked up the imaginary receiver, her
expression became a delightful grin, and she turned to
me and exclaimed, "Do you know what Jesus said to

me? He said He loved me!" Hallelujah! Jesus introduced
into any situation brings healing.

Fear of Germs

Although this lady did not know where her fear
came from, another lady knew exactly when her
particular fear entered. She came for inner healing
because of fear of germs. Her husband came with her.

She shared that her fear of germs had become so
compulsive that she was constantly cleaning her house.
(Mentally I thought, "Oh, I'd like to borrow you for a
while!") She was constantly bathing their little
daughter, constantly washing off the door knobs,
cleaning the bathrooms. She even insisted that her
husband change clothes several times a day.

He said that her phobia was destroying their
marriage. A psychologist who was counseling with them
said that if she did not get better, the only alternative
would be divorce.

The Bible instructs us to forget the past and look
forward to what lies ahead; but obviously, the past is
not forgotten when a memory is still causing problems.
Jesus wants to cleanse the wounds, and take out all the
slivers of fear in the wound; then the wound will heal
properly and we can truly forget the past.

The wife shared the incident that had caused this
fear of germs which eventually brought on compulsive
hand-washing. She was pregnant at a time when she and
her husband decided to visit relatives. They arrived at
their destination before the relatives had returned from
their vacation.

A member of the family, who was slightly
brain-damaged, was supposed to be taking care of the

house, but he had left also. Several dogs had been locked up in the house, and dog excrement was everywhere. Coupled with the odor and the heat was the fear for the whereabouts of the family member who was supposed to be taking care of the house.

Emotions and feelings ran rampant, and the repulsion of this experience grew and grew until it became a devastating, overpowering compulsion. She was overwhelmed with the constant feeling of being dirty and unclean.

When we prayed for inner healing for this couple, the power of the Lord going through them was so strong, a person standing by them said later, "You know, I could almost feel electricity, the power of the Lord was so evident!" Some time later, I received word that she had been set free completely from this fear. Thank You, Lord Jesus!

Fears of Suffocating and Swallowing

My husband received a word from the Lord in a meeting that someone was being set free from the fear of suffocation. Immediately, a lady started weeping for joy. She explained that when she was a child, her daddy would playfully put a pillow over her head. This "supposedly" innocent game had left her with a deep-seated fear of being unable to breathe. But praise God! She was set free that night. She said that when God touched her, it was as though a weight was lifted. Some fears affect us physically as well as emotionally. A lady in Canada had not been able to swallow solid foods for twenty years, but in a group inner healing meeting the Lord healed the fear that caused the feeling she had of always having a knot in her throat.

The Lord had given me a word of knowledge that He was healing someone who had trouble swallowing. The lady came back to the meeting the next night to share that she had gone home and eaten solid food. She had been set free from the fear, which also eliminated the physical or psychosomatic problem. Praise the Lord!

The Story of Don*

It's not just women and children that Satan sends fears against. He is no respecter of persons and comes against men with fear in the same way.

The president of a women's group that had invited me to speak said, "Betty, I really believe you're here not just to speak to our group, but I believe the Lord has you here to pray with my husband for inner healing."

"Well, praise the Lord; what's the problem?" I asked.

"For one thing," she said, "he is so filled with fear — almost uncontrollable at times. Also, there is a broken relationship with his mother. In fact, she is in the hospital and has been there for several days, and he won't go to see her or call her. He says, 'Why should I check on her? She never did anything for me.'" The wife continued, "My husband can be so sweet, but at

*Name has been changed

times there almost seems to be two different people in him."

I agreed that I would pray with her husband if the Lord led in that direction, and also if the husband wanted inner healing. Because of the tremendously tight schedule, we agreed that if the Lord wanted me to pray with him, He would have to provide the time, because almost every moment was taken.

Late that night, as the wife and husband and I were visiting in their family room, it was as if the Lord spoke to her and to me at the same time. She got up and walked out of the room saying, "I must do some things for the meeting in the morning." I think we both knew the Lord was saying, "Now is the time to pray for Don."

There is always an inner excitement, an inner knowing when you can sense that God is directing and has something that He is getting ready to do. At times like this our only problem is to stay out of His way and let Him do it. We must not run ahead and foul up His plans.

I asked the husband about his job; he was a successful businessman. Though I kept the conversation light, I noticed that he was very non-committal, and his nervousness was very evident. Even in a normal conversation, his eyes would dart back and forth in fear.

As we continued to talk, he asked about the book on inner healing that I had written. I shared that God wanted us to be whole — spirit, soul, and body, and that the two steps of inner healing were (1) binding

Satan's negative forces that he sends against us, and I named a few; and (2) asking Jesus to heal all painful memories. He said, "You know, I've always had this fear, and also I don't have the inner peace that I need." Then he began to share his story:

For some reason my parents took me to live with my grandparents when I was just a little boy. There were other children in my family, but I was the only one they did not keep. Even without realizing it, the seed of rejection had been planted.

I loved my grandmother dearly; in fact, she was just like a mother to me. After my grandfather died, my grandmother and I became even closer. There was an unmarried son who lived with her, and this became my family unit.

I was twelve when my grandmother developed cancer. I was the one who went with her for her daily treatments. The sounds and the odors were overwhelming to me as a twelve-year-old. In some way I felt solely responsible for my grandmother's recovery.

For the next five years, I was the one who cleansed the cancer sores and changed the dressings at home. Besides the fear breeding way down inside of me, along with the rejection that was already

growing, resentment was creeping in. I
constantly faced the unanswered
question, God, why did You allow this
to happen?

My grandmother died when I was
seventeen, and my entire world crumbled
around me. The only family I knew,
loved, and felt close to was gone.

As I listened to his story it seemed the verse in Job
3:25 applied just to him, *"What I always feared has
happened to me."* He said that the week after his
grandmother was buried, the uncle who lived with him
married and moved away. At the age of seventeen he
was completely on his own.

The seeds planted by Satan found fertile soil. The
door that had been opened when rejection came in now
made it easier for bitterness, anger, and rage to enter.
The hostility he felt of being all alone grew and grew.

He continued his story: "Success became my one
goal. 'I will succeed! I will show the world! I will
become somebody;' I kept saying to myself."

After he married, God still did not have a place in
their marriage. Then one day his wife accepted Jesus as
her personal Savior. She became "on fire" for the Lord.
She knew that God had a plan for her and for her
husband, but Satan had such a strong hold on his life.

There were times when in a rage he would actually
choke her; other times when she would be away from
home, fear would overwhelm him, and he would call
her to have her pray with him. He slept with a gun
under his pillow.

Fear was such a part of his life, he constantly looked over his shoulder to see if anyone was following him. His wife shared with me earlier that just two nights before I came to their home, she was at a state convention meeting. While she was away, her husband was in bed when he sensed an evil presence enter the room.

He was so terrified, and the presence was so real, that he actually called his dog to "scare" away whatever "thing" he was encountering. He phoned his wife across the state to have her pray with him.

As he finished his story, he paused and I said, "God wants to set you free. He wants to heal you. He wants to fill you with His love; and remember, God's perfect love will cast out all fear (see I John 4:18 KJV).

He said, "You know, I believe that, and I'd like for you to pray with me." So we knelt down, he by his chair, and I by the sofa. (His wife was praying fervently in the adjoining room.)

Praise the Lord for His promise that whatever you bind on earth is bound in heaven (see Matthew 18:18). The Lord completely set him free from all negative forces: fear, suspicion, bitterness, resentment, pride, anger, jealousy, rejection, rage, insecurity, and hatred. After we finished praying for the healing of his memories, he quickly went to his wife and gave her a great big hug.

Later his wife shared, "I knew a miracle had taken place when he very gently asked me to forgive him for all the hurt he had caused me." Then, the next day, he called his mother and talked to her in the hospital. The

miracle of reconciliation had begun. The wife laughed
and said, "You know, I really knew the Lord had
touched him when he enjoyed visiting with my mother,
who came the next day."

Surely, this is the principle the Lord had in mind in
Eph. 2:15 *"Then he took the two groups that had been
opposed to each other and made them parts of himself;
thus he fused us together to become one new person
and at last there was peace."* What God starts He
completes. This was just the beginning of the work in
his life. It was the beginning of a spiritual pilgrimage. In
a very short time, he surrendered his life to God's call
to the ministry. He resigned from his position, and the
last time I saw him and his wife, they were both
planning to enter a Bible school.

Are you filled with fear? God loves you so much. He
wants you to be filled with peace and joy,
holy-boldness, confidence, assurance. He did not create
you to be bowed down with fear and anxiety. If you
have fears of any kind: rejection, darkness, illness, death,
failure, driving, going into crowds, water, animals,
insects, snakes, people, speaking in public, flying, closed
places, heights, choking, germs, — whatever your fear is,
God wants to set you free.

There is not one thing any person can do to heal
you, but God can. Jesus paid the price on Calvary to
cover your feelings of fear, anxiety, hypertension,
worry, panic, nervousness. Can you trust Him? Can you
believe that He does want to set you free, that He does
want to heal you?

Would you pray this prayer with me, and remember that it is the power of Jesus that heals. We give all the praise and glory to Him.

PRAYER TO BE SET FREE FROM FEAR

Lord Jesus, I know Your Word says You did not give us a spirit of fear, but of power, love, and a sound mind. Thank You that because of Your shed blood I can be set free.

Satan, I bind you from me in the name of Jesus. I bind and cast out in the name of Jesus the spirit of fear and all related spirits.

Please, Jesus, heal the memory of the experience that allowed this fear to enter. I ask that You set me free from anxiety, tension, nervousness. Help me to remember, "He that is in me is greater than he that is in the world." Remind me, dear Lord, that if You are for me who can be against me.

Please fill me with Your perfect love. Fill me with Your calmness, Your peace, Your joy. Give me holy boldness and the assurance that I can do all things through Christ who strengthens me. I put my trust in You, God. Thank You, dear Jesus, for healing me. I give You all the praise and glory. It is in the name of Jesus I pray. Amen.

Scriptures Related To Fear

II Timothy 1:7 KJV "For God hath not given us the spirit of fear; but of power, and of love, and of a sound mind."

I John 4:18 KJV "There is no fear in love; but perfect love casteth out fear; because fear hath torment. He that feareth is not made perfect in love."

Luke 12:32 "So don't be afraid, little flock . . ."

Isaiah 41:10 "Fear not, for I am with you. Do not be dismayed. I am your God. I will strengthen you; I will help you; I will uphold you with My victorious right hand."

Isaiah 12:2 ". . . I will trust and not be afraid, for the Lord is my strength and song; he is my salvation."

Psalm 46:1,2 "God is our refuge and strength, a tested help in times of trouble. And so we need not fear even if the world blows up, and the mountains crumble into the sea."

Psalm 91:5 "Now you don't need to be afraid of the dark any more nor fear the dangers of the day."

Isaiah 41:13 "I am holding you by your right hand — I, the Lord your God — and I say to you, Don't be afraid; I am here to help you."

Psalm 27:1 "The Lord is my light and my salvation; whom shall I fear?"

Hebrews 13:6 "That is why we can say without any doubt or fear, "The Lord is my Helper and I am not afraid of anything that mere man can do to me."

Psalm 56:10,11 "I am trusting God — oh, praise his promises! I am not afraid of anything mere man can do to me! Yes, praise his promises."

Exodus 14:13 "Don't be afraid. Just stand where you are and watch, and you will see the wonderful way the Lord will rescue you today . . ."

Proverbs 1:33 "But all who listen to me shall live in peace and safety, unafraid."

Isaiah 35:4 "Encourage those who are afraid. Tell them, 'Be strong, fear not, for your God is coming to destroy your enemies. He is coming to save you.' "

Deuteronomy 31:8 "Don't be afraid, for the Lord will go before you and will be with you; he will not fail nor forsake you."

Psalms 112:7 "He does not fear bad news, nor live in dread of what may happen. For he is settled in his mind that Jehovah will take care of him."

Isaiah 43:2,3 "When you go through deep waters and great trouble, I will be with you. When you go through rivers of difficulty, you will not drown! When you walk through the fire of oppression, you will not be burned up — the flames will not consume you. For I am the Lord your God, your Savior . . ."

Psalms 118:6 "He is for me! How can I be afraid? What can mere man do to me? The Lord is on my side, he will help me. Let those who hate me beware."

Psalms 121:6-8 "He protects you day and night. He keeps you from all evil, and preserves your life. He keeps his eye upon you as you come and go, and always guards you."

John 14:27 "I am leaving you a gift — peace of mind and heart! And the peace I give isn't fragile like the peace the world gives. So don't be troubled or afraid."

Chapter Three

SET FREE FROM NIGHTMARES

A fear that is so grievous is fear of the dark, and related to this fear is the fear of going to sleep or the fear that causes nightmares. The Lord wants His beloved to have their rest, and usually, the rest comes as we sleep. It is Satan who comes against us as we sleep.

He comes against even God's people by instilling the fear of the dark, by sending imaginary sounds and noises, or by sending nightmares. He may cause your heart to "pound" or your skin to "crawl" as you wait for the blessed sleep to come.

He is the one who makes your mind race with thoughts of all the things that might happen, or of all the things left undone. He comes against children and adults alike with nightmares — and they are nerve-wracking whatever your age. But God is so faithful He wants to heal that area of our lives, too.

I remember a little first grader who had not wanted to come for prayer. The appointment was for 2:30 on a Monday afternoon, and that meant she would have to

miss her Brownie meeting. But since this was the only
time available, her parents insisted that she come. They
were very concerned over her recurring nightmares.

She was a beautiful, intelligent little girl, who had
invited Jesus into her heart even at this young age. Her
parents were Spirit-filled Christians.

We all knelt by the sofa to pray together. I told her
to picture Jesus in her mind. Then I began to pray for
her. In a few minutes, this wiggly, fidgety little girl
became very, very still. She remained that way for
fifteen minutes, until I finished praying for her. I
wondered if she was asleep.

Later, the mother asked her if she had been sleeping.
"No, Mother," she answered. "I heard everything you
were saying, but I felt so funny." The "funny" feeling
was obviously the healing power of the Lord.

The family lived in Texas when I prayed with the
little girl. They have since moved to Hawaii. Here is the
mother's letter:

> When Melissa was about five and a half
> years old, she began having bad dreams
> two or three nights a week. The dreams
> were always about vampires of the
> Dracula variety, something we believe
> she saw on a children's television pro-
> gram.
>
> Of course, we prayed with her and
> also made certain that she never watched
> that program; however, the dreams con-
> tinued. During that year, we continued
> to search for the cause of the dreams.

The Lord is so faithful to give us wisdom if we seek solutions from Him.

We discovered that our church children's program had been putting an undue emphasis on Satan and demons, and we felt that this had had a decided influence on Melissa to the point of contributing to the nightmare situation.

My husband and I counseled with an elder of our church who recommended that we take Melissa to you. On the afternoon of the appointment, Melissa was somewhat apprehensive, but as you talked with her in your gentle way, she began to respond. You read some Scriptures from the Psalms concerning sleep, and then you told her we would all kneel by your sofa and ask Jesus to take away these bad dreams.

When you finished praying and the three of us raised our heads, our daughter did not. I had noticed that Melissa's breathing became more relaxed as soon as you began to pray. It was then, after prayer, that we realized she supposedly had been "asleep" throughout our prayer time. The only explanation we have for an active six-year-old girl falling "asleep" in mid-afternoon, during only a few minutes of prayer, is that she had been under the power of

God. Our conclusion was made more definite by her remark to me that evening: "I didn't know what you all were saying, Mama, but I could hear your voices."

The result is that since that afternoon six months ago, Melissa has had only one other dream about a vampire, and she told us the next morning that she was not even afraid. Praise the Lord for His tender love and concern for one small girl's problems.

The previous testimony came from Hawaii; the following one comes from Canada.

The morning after ministering in Saskatchewan, Canada, my husband Ed and I were counseling with a family of four who had attended the meeting the night before. The first thing the father said as he turned to his ten-year-old son was, "Tell Mrs. Tapscott what happened last night."

The boy said, "Well, I broke my ankle a year ago and then re-injured it three weeks ago. But last night the Lord took all the pain away at the meeting. Not only that, but the Lord also healed me of the fear of darkness."

The mother added to his testimony that no one really knew when the fear entered, but the evidence of the fear was that he walked through the house off and on all night. Going from one room to another, he would sleep a little while in one room and sleep for a while in another room. Praise the Lord! He healed him of that fear. His parents reported that he slept soundly all night long. Thank You, Jesus

Another mother said that after she divorced her husband, their eight-year-old son started having nightmares and evidence of other fears: of being sick, fears of germs, fears about school. She said that the main fear was of the dark and having nightmares.

When the door is open, Satan doesn't stop by sending just one giant against us. In this young boy's case, rejection probably was the first negative force to come against him. Then fears, insecurity, worry, inability to concentrate were added. Any traumatic change in a child's life can open the door for Satan to come against him.

The little boy didn't understand why he was having all the fears, but he knew he was miserable. He was afraid to go to school in the day time. At night he had horrible nightmares.

After Sunday services one morning, we prayed briefly, taking authority over the giants that had come against him and asking Jesus to heal the painful memories. We talked about the fact that God had stationed a guardian angel around him, and that Jesus was with him everywhere he went, whether it was at school, or when he was sleeping or playing.

A few weeks later when I saw this mother, she said that her son had been set free (almost completely) from his fears. Since inner healing is a continuing process, I shared with her how to pray the prayer for healing of memories with her son and ask God each day to fill the void in his life.

It's not only children who have nightmares; adults
can have them, too. Recently at a Christian Booksellers'
Convention, I talked with a lady, the mother of a good
friend, whom I had prayed with several years ago. She
said, "Betty, I have never had another nightmare since
the night you prayed."

This lady had been troubled with a recurring nightmare for four years. She was from another state but
had been in Houston visiting her daughter. They called
and asked for prayer for inner healing, hoping that God
would heal her of this recurring nightmare. When she
called, she asked if I interpreted dreams. I assured her
that I did not do that, but I surely would pray and ask
the Lord to set her free from her nightmares.

This was a Spirit-filled woman who loved the Lord
with all her heart, but Satan was coming against her to
rob her of her sleep. When she arrived, she described
the recurring dream. It was always the same. It started
very calmly as follows:

> I was in a car driving up to a beautiful
> house surrounded by huge, lovely trees.
> The house was very large and imposing;
> windows were everywhere. Because the
> house seemed so peaceful and cheerful, I
> happily climbed the steps to the porch.
> As I entered the house, the interesting
> layout and furnishings of the many
> rooms in the old-fashioned house thrilled
> me.
>
> In every dream, I found plenty of
> work to keep me busy. I would tirelessly

hang curtains, for instance, climbing up and down ladders in order to get the curtains to match and be the right length.

I was very happy as I worked alone during the bright, sunny, daylight hours. But as it began to grow dark, I began to panic. Rushing around madly, I frantically tried to lock every door, to check the locks on the many windows, and to pull down the blinds which never quite came down to the window sills. Dashing around the house, I found some locks I had missed; others were broken, or the keys were missing.

Meanwhile, faces were appearing and disappearing at the windows, and I heard noises outside. With each sound, my panic increased until I was close to hysteria.

There was a force that caused me to climb a certain staircase and enter a very dark room against my will. I didn't want to go there as I was so afraid. As I approached the room, I felt a thousand devils reaching out to catch my hand and pull me into the room. The terror was nearly more than I could bear.

I turned to run, stumbled, and fell down the steps. I began running through the dark maze of rooms searching for an outside door.

Then I would suddenly wake up so frightened, I was weak all over. I would lie there so grateful to realize I was in my own bed. I would wonder, "Why, Lord, have I had to dream this time after time?"

When I came to Betty's home for prayer, she dealt with me very tenderly. I tearfully related the memory of the recurring dream. Betty said, "Let's ask Jesus to walk through this house with you."

We both knelt by the sofa and with Jesus' help, we walked back through every step of the house, even up that forbidding stairwell and into that terrifying black room. She insisted that with Jesus accompanying me, I need have no fear. This took tremendous courage on my part to enter that room, but once I did, I was utterly amazed to find the room, while ebony black, to be totally empty. The great deceiver had kept me chained with fear of the horror of that room.

After I was able to face that dark room, the Lord later explained every detail of the dream to me, revealing earlier happenings in my personal life that had bearing on the nightmare. He completely freed me from every area of

my life that might cause this dream to
occur again.

It is eleven months now since Betty
prayed with me. I have never had the
dream again.

This delightful lady entered into the prayer for inner
healing so beautifully and completely. When I explained
the principle of introducing Jesus into every situation, I
asked her to picture Jesus walking up the stairs with
her. At one point in our prayer, fear came back against
her; and I reminded her that not only Jesus but His
guardian angels were with her. I said, "Picture Jesus; He
has your hand and the guardian angel is right in front
as the three of you climb those foreboding stairs." The
fear left instantly.

Her face broke out into a smile, and she said, "I can
just see that angel in my spirit, and his wings are
touching each side of the staircase." With Jesus and His
angels going with her she was not afraid of entering the
room that had been so terrifying to her. The moment
she walked (in her imagination) into the room she
realized that nothing − absolutely nothing − was in the
room, and she said, "Oh, thank You, Jesus. Praise, You
Jesus." Tears of joy streamed down her face as she
realized the great deceiver had been unmasked and she
was free. Praise the Lord!

Are you afraid of the dark? Do you dread for night
to come, for sleep to come, afraid you'll have nightmares? Do you sleep fretfully, hearing noises, creaking
stairs, imaginary burglars? Do you wake up exhausted
from a fear-spent night?

God didn't intend for your night to be that way. He wants His beloved to have their sleep, free from all fear and nightmares. God is as interested in that area of your life as in any other area.

Will you pray the following prayer and believe God to set you free and heal you:

PRAYER BEFORE YOU SLEEP

Lord Jesus, I thank You for Your day time and for Your night time. I know You never sleep but constantly watch over me. I know You have placed Your guardian angels all around me.

Lord, I give You all my cares and my worries of the day. I give You all my fears.

Satan, I bind you from me in the name of Jesus. All spirits of fear, especially fear of the dark, you are bound from me in the name of Jesus. I rebuke the fear of fire and fear of intruders in the name of Jesus. Spirits of insomnia, nervousness, tension, worry, I cast you out in the name of Jesus.

Lord, please go into the darkest recesses of my mind, into my subconscious, into the dream area, and heal all painful memories and trauma.

Lord, I ask You to fill me with Your divine love, Your peace, Your calmness. I pray You will allow me to sleep soundly all night long and wake up feeling refreshed in the morning. I commit myself to You.

It's in the name of Jesus that I pray. Amen.

WHAT PARENTS CAN DO TO PREVENT FEAR
FROM ENTERING A CHILD

In no way do I mean to heap guilt or condemnation on a parent. Many times I have heard people blaming a parent for their problems instead of letting Jesus give them an abundant life. They had their eyes on the problem instead of on the problem solver. However, there are some things that we can do as sensible parents to prevent Satan from sending fear against our children.

1. Censor very, very carefully the television shows your child watches. Even some of the so-called children's shows on Saturday morning can cause fear. Watch to see what your child is assimilating; watch for negative reactions. Does he become tense and hyperactive after watching a show? Does the show cause him to have bad dreams? Don't allow your child to listen to ghost stories.

2. Don't ever lock a child in a closet or a room for punishment.

3. Don't punish a child for being afraid (of the dark, for instance). It is a very real and valid fear to him, and only Jesus can heal that fear. Punishment only compounds the fear by adding rejection.

4. Don't say, "The policeman will get you if you're not nice." We need to instill respect and confidence for our law officers.

5. A child must learn safety precautions against petting strange dogs or cats, going into a street, going near deep water, riding with strangers, etc. But try to give your child a healthy respect for these things without instilling abnormal fear into him.

6. Take time to explain the thunder and lightning to a child who is frightened of storms. Talk about God's beautiful handiwork and power. Teach a child to take reasonable precautions such as not standing under trees during electrical storms.

7. Children should not be viewing monster movies or horror movies at all — ever! Halloween or no Halloween! You might say, "Why, I grew up on those, and I don't have fear." You may not, but another may grow up with fear buried way down in his subconscious. And is it worth it? "Garbage in, garbage out," as the computer lingo goes.

8. Be honest with your child. If you must go away on a trip, etc., explain it to him. Don't slip away. If the child must go to the doctor, hospital, or dentist, explain very carefully what will take place. Explain, "Yes, there may be some pain, but it won't last for long."

9. Tell your child every day that you love him. Don't allow the fear of rejection to enter by saying in jest (but really in anger), "I'm just going to give you away." I was shopping with a friend several years ago. Her little three-year-old boy kept acting up. Finally, in desperation she said, "I'm not going to love you anymore if you don't behave." Instantly you could see his attitude change, but not necessarily for the best. He started hanging onto her and saying, "Please love me, Mommy. I love you, Mommy. Love me, Mommy. Please, Mommy, love me." Show your child you love him by words and actions.

10. The moment your child has a terrifying experience, take time to pray with him right then. Don't

make fun of the child; don't say: "Big boys don't get frightened" or "Big girls don't cry." Ask the Lord Jesus to walk back and heal that terrifying experience. You may have to pray many times before the fear is gone. Talk with your child about the incident. Then you, as a parent, can pray for that child daily, asking the Lord to take a spiritual eraser and wipe away every memory of the fear, and to fill the void with His love and peace.

Scriptures To Help You Sleep

Psalm 3:5 "Then I lay down and slept in peace and woke up safely, for the Lord was watching over me."

Psalm 4:8 "I will lie down in peace and sleep, for though I am alone, O Lord, you will keep me safe."

Psalm 56:3,4 "But when I am afraid, I will put my confidence in you. Yes, I will trust the promises of God. And since I am trusting him, what can mere man do to me?"

Proverbs 3:24-26 "... you need not be afraid of disaster or the plots of wicked men, for the Lord is with you; he protects you."

Psalm 91:5,6 "Now you don't need to be afraid of the dark anymore, nor fear the dangers of the day; nor dread the plagues of darkness, nor disasters in the morning."

Chapter Four

SET FREE FROM GUILT

A 35-year-old lady came up to me when our inner healing meeting was over and asked for prayer. After almost everyone had left, we sat down on the church pew, and she shared her story with me.

Tears flooded her eyes as she began her story. When she was fourteen she became pregnant. Her boyfriend was fifteen. They were ashamed, afraid, and over-whelmed with fear and guilt. They felt they could not tell their parents. So in utter desperation, they decided to kill themselves.

After much discussion, they decided on the way to end their lives. The boy would steal a car, and they would drive in front of a train. The appointed night came. The boy stole the car and came to pick up the girl.

But — on that particular night, she was babysitting her two-year-old brother. As only a fourteen-year-old would reason, she said, "I can't go kill myself. I have to babysit." The boy was adamant and angry. He'd already stolen the car. The plans were all made; but she would not leave the little two-year-old by himself.

So the boyfriend picked up her best girl friend and he completed the horrendous suicide plans he had made. In the stolen car he ran in front of a train; he and the girl were both killed.

The grown lady sobbed as she shared this heartbreaking story. "A few months later I had my baby, but it died," she said, as she brushed a tear from her cheek. "I grew up and married. In later years I became a Christian, was even filled with the Spirit; but, all my life, I've suffered from fear, guilt, and such condemnation."

"Everytime I come to a railroad crossing, I'm overcome with guilt. I think of my boyfriend and the girlfriend that died in my place. I'm so terrified of being hit by a train, that I stop the car and have to work up courage to drive across the tracks."

"Or I sometimes speed rapidly across the tracks, trying not to think of my past. If my husband stops too close to the approaching train, I almost go into hysterics, afraid he is going to roll onto the tracks and into the path of a fast approaching train."

She asked without expecting an answer, "Do you have any idea how many railroad crossings I go across everyday?" She paused a moment, and then she had another question. "Do you think I can be healed of this horrible fear and guilt?"

You see, Satan is not content in just sending one spirit against us. Once the door is open through sin, and once he gets his foot in the door, he brings as many of his negative forces against us as he can. He didn't stop with the main force of guilt in this lady's case; he also sent fear.

I shared with her that I believed when she introduced Jesus into the situation, He most definitely would heal her painful memories and set her free from her fear and guilt.

I reminded her that Isaiah 43:25 says, "... *I alone am he who blots away your sins for my own sake and will never think of them again.*" "But remember," I continued, "when you are set free, it is because Jesus sets you free, and for no other reason. He gets all the praise and glory."

We bound the spirits of guilt, condemnation, shame, embarrassment, fear, remorse, and grief in the name of Jesus. Then we asked Him to take a spiritual eraser and wipe this painful memory from her mind and to fill her with His presence. We invited Him into each situation

I asked her to picture Jesus driving with her in the car, and to know that His angels were stationed all about her car. I prayed that Jesus would flood her with His love, joy, and peace.

The next night, she came back to the meeting and said, "Praise the Lord, I've been healed!" Excitedly she exclaimed, "Today, everytime I went across any railroad crossings, the railroad sign looked just like a *cross* to me. And there was Jesus standing right there with His arms folded. Oh! He set me free from that horrible fear and guilt." Isn't it absolutely glorious what God can do? Praise His glorious name!

One New Year's Day, when I answered the phone, a man gave his name and the state from which he was

calling. He said, "I so desperately need prayer," and
then he started crying. In between sobs he kept saying,
"I've lost my salvation. I've done something so horrible,
I will never be forgiven." I could barely understand
what he was saying as he kept pouring out his anguish
over the sin he had committed.

Finally, I asked, "Sir, what is it you have done?"
Frankly, I almost expected a confession of a mass
murder or something as horrendous.

In broken sentences he sobbed, "I stole some money
from my employer. I'm a Christian, and I knew better.
I just know God will not forgive me."

"Have you asked forgiveness for all your sins and
invited Jesus into your heart as your personal Savior?"

"Yes, I have," he said. "I invited Jesus into my heart
a long time ago, but I belong to a church that teaches
us if you sin, you stand the chance of losing your
salvation."

This book certainly is not one on doctrine, but the
Bible says in Hebrews 10:17, *". . . I will never again
remember their sins and lawless deeds."* Romans 8:1
declares, *"So there is now no condemnation awaiting
those who belong to Christ Jesus."* This does not give
us the license to sin any time we want to, but if we
stumble, if we fall, if we sin either by ommission or
commission, by attitude or action, God's Word says
that He will forgive if we humble ourselves and ask
forgiveness.

I went over the Scriptures with this man and assured
him that if he had asked Jesus into his heart, if he had
asked forgiveness for stealing the money and had made
restitution, then he was *forgiven.*

He stopped crying long enough to say, "Well, I borrowed some money and took it back to my employer, and my employer said I didn't owe him anything, that I was forgiven. I asked my family to forgive me, and they said I was forgiven also. Then he paused and with a deep, heart-rending sob, said, "I can't forgive myself. I can't accept God's forgiveness."

Actually, when this happens, we are playing God. We are not allowing God to be the judge, but we are judging ourselves. I Corinthians 4:3,4 KJV says that we are to let God judge us. We cannot "earn" salvation; we cannot "earn" forgiveness. Jesus paid the price for us long ago. The Bible says in Titus 3:5, *"then he saved us — not because we were good enough to be saved, but because of his kindness and pity — by washing away our sins and giving us the new joy of the indwelling Holy Spirit."*

Emily Gardner Neal in *The Healing Power of Christ* wrote,

> It is a curious paradox that the Christian, who of all people knows the source of forgiveness, should at the same time suffer so greatly from feelings of guilt. This must continually hurt the heart of God, for it actually negates our Lord's sacrifice on the cross for our sins.

Satan had come against this man in a weak moment. He had stolen the money. Then Satan continued to come against him, not only with guilt and condemnation, but with the fear of losing his salvation.

But praise God, we have power over the enemy. We can be rescued from Satan's bondage. God's Word says,

*"For he has rescued us out of the darkness and gloom
of Satan's kingdom and brought us into the kingdom of
his dear Son, who bought our freedom with his blood
and forgave us all our sins" (Colossians 1:13,14).*

I read the verse from Romans 10:9, *"For if you tell
others with your own mouth that Jesus Christ is your
Lord, and believe in your own heart that God has
raised him from the dead, you will be saved."* I had the
man reaffirm his commitment to Jesus:

> I know Jesus died on the cross for me. I
> know He has forgiven me of all my sins.
> I know He is my Savior. I know His
> word is true, and that He no longer
> remembers my sins and lawless deeds. I
> know I am forgiven. Thank You, Jesus,
> for being my Savior. Thank You for
> Your forgiveness. It is in Your name I
> pray. Amen.

Praise God, time and space mean nothing to Jesus.
God's power went out across those telephone wires that
morning to a far away state as we took authority over
the negative forces coming against the man. I asked him
to repeat after me:

> Satan, you are bound from me in the
> name of Jesus. Spirits of guilt and con-
> demnation, you are bound and cast out
> in the name of Jesus. Spirits of fear and
> doubt, you are bound in the name of
> Jesus. Spirits of self-hatred and embar-
> rassment, you are bound and cast out in
> the name of Jesus. Spirits of depression

and suicide, you are bound and cast out
in the name of Jesus.

At one point in the prayer, I could actually feel the oppression lifting. Obviously, the man could feel it, too, because he started crying again, but this time, for joy. He started to shout and praise God as the liberating power of Jesus broke the chains of bondage and set him free. *"So if the Son sets you free, you will indeed be free" (John 8:36).*

We finished praying by asking the Lord to heal every hurt caused by the embarrassment, guilt, and shame, and to fill him with His love, joy, and peace. The joy of his salvation was restored to him (see Psalm 51:13). Praise the Lord!

At one group meeting on inner healing, the Lord seemed to say that a woman there had a feeling of guilt because of the death of someone, but that she was being set free from this guilt. I was amazed when six people came up after the meeting, each saying, "I was that person, and the Lord has set me free."

One person said, "My dad died when I was fifteen. I was a Christian, but I never did share Jesus with him. He was not a believer when he died."

Another person said, "I have always had guilt because I did not take my elderly mother to a meeting where they were praying for the sick. I've always said, "If only I had taken her, perhaps she would have been healed."

"I didn't realize," another person said, "that my child was as sick as he was, and I didn't get him to the doctor soon enough; my child died. Oh, the guilt I've had all these years." The other three ladies had similar stories.

Satan comes against us at our weakest moments when our hearts are broken with grief. Then he adds other weights of guilt and condemnation. All these ladies said that Jesus had set them free and they went away rejoicing.

A young woman called long distance one day saying that she felt so far away from God. She was a Christian and attended church regularly. I kept questioning her to find the reason she felt alienated from God. She had not been involved in the occult, and she said there was no one whom she had not forgiven. But she kept saying, "I don't feel the fullness of the Lord."

I explained that we don't go by feelings, but by faith. Dr. Gilbert Little in *The Christian and Emotional Problems* says:

> Feelings have absolutely nothing to do with our salvation or forgiveness of past sins. We know we are saved because of God's promises, which cannot be broken. The Bible tells us, *"Believe on the Lord Jesus Christ, and thou shalt be saved:"* (*Acts 16:31*).
>
> The Word of God does not promise that we will "feel" as if we are saved. Instead, it states the simple fact that we are saved when we fulfill God's condition: *"That whosoever believeth in him (God's only begotten Son) should not perish, but have everlasting life"* (*John 3:16 KJV*).

When we repent of our sins, confess them to God and turn from them, we have the promise of God's forgiveness: *'If we confess our sins, he is faithful and just to forgive us our sins, and to cleanse us from all unrighteousness' (I John 1:9 KJV).*

God's promises have nothing to do with our feelings. When God forgives us He is satisfied about our forgiven sins. Therefore, we should be satisfied and not doubt by looking for a sign, in this case a "feeling." Faith is opposite of feeling. *"Faith is . . . the evidence of things not seen" (Heb. 11:1 KJV).* It is the evidence of things not felt.

I knew what the young woman was trying to say. Something was still standing in her way of being a joyous, Spirit-filled Christian. When I prayed, she received a measure of relief. But just a few days later she called long distance the second time saying, "Please pray for me again. Something is wrong. I just can't seem to reach God. Something is blocking me."

Fervently, I asked God to reveal to me what was holding this young woman back from receiving all God had to offer. He seemed to be saying the word "abortion." Now, she had never mentioned an abortion, but gently I asked, "Have you had an abortion?"

It was as if the dam burst. She started sobbing as if her heart would break. "Yes," she said, "I did have an abortion, and I can't get over the guilt and condemnation. I just can't forgive myself. I can't accept God's forgiveness."

"Have you asked forgiveness from God?" I asked.

"Yes," she said, "so many, many times."

"Oh," I said, "don't you know that Jesus has already forgiven you and that the slate is clean?"

"Yes," she said, "with my intellect I know it, but I can't get it down into my spirit."

So we took authority over the negative forces that Satan was sending against her — spirits of guilt, condemnation, shame, remorse, self-hatred, murder, unforgiveness, and so on. Then we asked the Lord to heal all the hurts this experience had caused.

We asked Him to take a spiritual eraser and wipe away the painful memories of the abortion. I could feel the healing power of the Lord sweep over her as He took the oil of the Holy Spirit and cleansed those deep, deep wounds. She felt such peace and cleansing as she accepted God's forgiveness and forgave herself.

I heard from her one more time. She told me that she felt like a different person. She had been filled with the Holy Spirit and the joy of the Lord.

False Guilt

There are two types of guilt: false guilt and real guilt. False guilt can be just as damaging as real guilt. Cecil Osborn in *The Art of Understanding Yourself* says:

> False guilt refers to our feelings of guilt
> where there is no actual guilt, either of

commission or omission. One may not
have knowingly violated any law of God
or man and yet experience a deep sense
of guilt. This false guilt usually stems
from such things as rejection in childhood, causing the child to feel unwanted, unloved, and therefore worthless. This may persist through life in
some diffused indefinable form. The
individual is not sure whether to call it a
sense of guilt, inferiority, inadequacy,
shame, or alienation. He simply feels
vaguely "worthless," "no good," a
"reject." Each of these feelings registers
on the unconscious mind as guilt.

As a child, you may have been told (no matter how
much you studied), "If you'd only studied more, you
would have made better grades." So you ended up
feeling guilty for not studying harder. Or perhaps at
your piano recital, you played to the best of your
ability, but you still made mistakes. Someone said,
"Well, you should have practiced more," and you felt
guilt and condemnation for not having practiced longer
hours.

A parent must admonish and discipline a child, but it
has to be done in love and gentleness, and sprinkled
with a generous amount of praise.

I witnessed a mother-daughter scene in a store
recently. The child had committed some childish in-
fraction, and in anger, the mother shook her and
spanked her. Then she screeched at her as they stood in

line to check out. The mother kept looking at the little
girl with a withering stare that said, "You're bad,
you're naughty, and I don't love you."

I wonder if the little girl will grow up with a high
level of guilt. Will she become a student who thinks the
teacher is suspecting her of cheating on a test when the
teacher just looks her way? Or will she be a person who
will grow up and feel guilty when a store clerk looks at
her in a suspicious way, even though she would never,
never steal an item from the store?

A person with a high level of false guilt will always
be the first to think, "I'm at fault in this argument."
Or if something goes wrong at home, he will automatically think, "Now, what did *I* do wrong?" He will
experience much condemnation and lack of self-esteem.

Is there a person who doesn't automatically look at
his speedometer when he hears the police siren behind
him — even when he knows he is not speeding? This
reaction is related to guilt.

When you were a youngster yourself, were you ever
near a baby, and for no apparent reason, it started
crying, as if in pain? You hadn't even touched it, but
the mother said, "Did you pinch that baby?" Even
though you denied it, the mother thought you were
guilty, and you *felt* guilty.

Some parents constantly teach guilt and condemnation either by word or facial expression. Verbally or
non-verbally, they tell their children, "You're bad;
you're naughty; you're ugly; you're a failure."

As parents, we need to praise our children, tell them
we love them, forgive them immediately, and teach

them to forgive themselves and to accept God's forgiveness, as well as our forgiveness.

Some ministers preach "hell-fire and damnation," guilt and condemnation from the pulpit, and the parishioner feels worse when he leaves the church than when he entered.

Don't misunderstand me. We must feel guilt when we have committed a sin. That is why the Lord gave us a conscience. We must be convicted of our sins, but once we have asked forgiveness and made restitution, we do not have to keep going back to the altar time after time confessing the same sin. When we do this, obviously we are not accepting God's forgiveness, and are still bowed down with false guilt.

Real Guilt

Real guilt comes in the aftermath of an experience in which someone has actually broken the law — if it's God's law, it's sin; if it's man's law, it is called a crime.

Adam and Eve were the first people to suffer from feelings of real guilt. After they had eaten the forbidden fruit, God walked into the garden, and they hid from Him. God asked, "Where are you?" Adam replied, *"... I heard thy voice in the garden, and I was afraid, because I was naked; and I hid myself" (Genesis 3:10 KJV)*.

Do you recall what Judas Iscariot did after he betrayed Jesus? He hung himself because he was completely overcome with guilt.

In His ministry, Jesus encountered many whose sicknesses were caused by real guilt, and He dealt with the

root cause of the problems. When friends let the young
man down through the roof, Jesus knew his paralysis
was the result of some past sin. He forgave the man and
healed him.

Not all sickness is caused by a past sin, and many
times Jesus pointed this out. He made it very plain
when that question was asked about the blind man.
Jesus said, *". . . Neither hath this man sinned, nor his
parents; but that the works of God should be made
manifest in him" (John 9:3 KJV).*

Dr. Quintin Hyder said in *The Christian's Handbook
of Psychiatry* that over half of his Christian patients
have guilt as part of their symptom complex. He wrote:

> Physical illness is often considered a
> form of punishment, a product of guilt
> feelings about some wrong-doing in the
> past. Some failure, dishonesty, laziness,
> thoughtlessness, lack of love, or selfish
> act — chronically infecting the mind and
> emotions from years back — leads to
> guilt feelings which cripple and even
> destroy a person's peace within. All
> these can not only cause physical illness
> but prevent its cure when it is seen as
> punishment. If the physical pain is in
> fact removed by medical treatment,
> another one will develop shortly after-
> ward. Psychologically and emotionally it
> is easier to tolerate the physical pain
> than the burden of guilt which has
> thereby been repressed.

It was thrilling to read what a noted Christian medical doctor and therapist had to say about guilt. Dr. Hyder also wrote:

> Any psychological theory which denies the Biblical concept that there is in fact a divine standard for man's behavior is limited in its therapeutic effectiveness precisely because it is virtually impossible to forget about serious past guilt-provoking transgressions. The memory is a stubborn part of the mind. To try and forget past wrongdoing cannot be done. Only forgiveness can give peace.

Many times, if a person cannot accept God's forgiveness, he will unconsciously try to punish himself. This may be the reason why some people are always having accidents or making wrong and bad choices.

One middle-aged lady who could not overcome her guilt feelings punished herself mentally. She had suffered a complete emotional collapse because of guilt. Her husband had committed adultery while he was drunk. To get even, she too, commited adultery. But the wife was a Christian, even a Sunday School teacher, and the sin she had committed just overwhelmed her. She could not accept God's forgiveness. She couldn't forgive herself, and she couldn't forgive her husband. The price of guilt in her case was a nervous breakdown. She escaped into a world of silence. She would not speak. When she was brought to our inner healing meeting, she could not even say the name "Jesus." She only stared off into space.

I had the husband bring her back the next day for in-depth prayer for the healing of memories. I bound the spirit of guilt in the name of Jesus. Slowly and gently I had her repeat after me, "Satan, you are bound from me in the name of Jesus." It took a long, long time just to get her to the point of being able to say those words. Gradually, she made it through the prayer of inner healing. Then she said haltingly, "But I was a Sunday School teacher. I was a Sunday School teacher."

I reminded her that Jesus had forgiven her. I quoted the Scripture concerning the woman taken in adultery in which Jesus said, ". . . *Neither do I condemn thee: go, and sin no more" (John 8:11 KJV)*. I told her, "You are forgiven. You are free. God's Word says He will never again remember your sins or lawless deeds" (see Hebrews 10:17).

At the end of two hours, this precious woman was able to say, "He that is in me is greater than he that is in the world " (see I John 4:4 KJV) and "I can do all things through Christ who strengthens me." (see Philippians 4:13 KJV).

When I asked the husband to come back into the room, they stood facing each other. You could see love and forgiveness reflected in their eyes. There was a new look of responsiveness in the wife's eyes. Tears rolled down her face.

I have not heard from this lady again. I do not know if she was able to walk on to complete victory or not. I pray that she was able to continue to accept the fact that she truly had been forgiven. But there was victory evident on her face that day as God's healing power flowed through her.

Dr. Bruce Narramore and Bill Counts in their book, *Guilt and Freedom,* wrote:

> One of the easiest — but most painful — ways to handle guilt feelings is to give up and become depressed. We accept guilt's accusation and feel rotten. When this happens, it becomes very difficult to function properly. The fear of punishment, sense of worthlessness, or feeling of rejection places a heavy burden on our emotional lives and drains us of energy we could otherwise spend on constructive endeavors. People who have surrendered to feelings of guilt and self-depreciation usually become chronically depressed.
>
> Guilt has a way of binding us down, of pressuring us, and of robbing us of freedom and spontaneity. And none of us is entirely free of guilt's influence. The perfectionist housewife; the worrier; the aggressive, driven businessman; the insomniac; the straight-"A" student; and the searching religious person are all partially motivated by hidden guilt. Each is trying something to develop a sense of self-acceptance or inner harmony . . . .

If a person is bowed down with guilt, Satan is not content until he sends many other forces against him:

depression, self-hatred, and sometimes even feelings of suicide.

One lady from Virginia wrote after we had prayer for inner healing over the telephone:

> I praise the Lord for delivering me from self-hate and self-condemnation, shame, and embarrassment. Praise the Lord for deliverance from a spirit of criticism, a judgmental spirit, doubt, and unbelief. Praise the Lord for taking from this house the spirit of darkness.
>
> Betty, as you prayed with me over the phone, as you prayed for self-hate, it was just like Satan didn't want to loose me from that sin. Then, the cleansing started with tears and a release came from the Lord. Oh, glory! Hallelujah! It really hurts, but what a good hurt when you know you are being made holy for God.
>
> I stand before the mirror now and look at myself and say, "I love you. I love You, Heavenly Father." I do this about five times each day. It is not easy to say, "I love you" to myself, but I know I must continue to work at self-love in a holy way.
>
> Jesus is the only psychiatrist who can and does heal body, soul (mind) and spirit.
>
> Betty, thank you from the bottom of my heart for praying with me. Your

empathy, understanding, and faith in
God are just priceless.

*"What happiness for those whose guilt has been
forgiven! What joys when sins are covered over! What
relief for those who have confessed their sins and God
has cleared their record" (Psalm 32:1,2).*

Are you bowed down with guilt and condemnation?
Do you feel that God could never forgive you? Can you
not forgive yourself? Jesus has already paid the price.
I John 1:9 says, *"But if we confess our sins to him, he
can be depended on to forgive us and to cleanse us
from every wrong . . ."*

Remember The Steps to Overcoming Guilt are:

1.   Be honest with yourself concerning the sin committed and the guilt felt.

2.   Confess the sin to God and ask His forgiveness.

3.   If you have hurt another, ask his forgiveness.

4.   Make restitution:

    a.   Pay back the money stolen, etc.

    b.   Replace the broken item (if possible).

    c.   Try to stop the gossip you started.

5.   Accept the fact that you may have to suffer the
consequences of your sin. Some things can never be
changed or done over.

6.   But also know that God has forgiven you, and
He wants you to forgive yourself, too.

7.   Pray or have someone pray with you, taking
authority over the giants of guilt coming against you.

8.   Pray that God will heal every painful memory
concerning the episode that brought about the guilt
feelings. Ask Him to help you forget the past and look
forward to what lies ahead.

PRAYER TO BE SET FREE FROM GUILT

Father, I thank You for Jesus who died on the cross for my sins and for my guilt. Satan, you are bound from me in the mighty name of Jesus. Jesus, please set me free from all the negative forces of guilt, condemnation, shame, embarrassment, self-hatred, unworthiness, and unforgiveness.

Dear Jesus, please wipe away every painful memory concerning the sin I committed, or the accident I caused, or the mistake I made. Please cleanse and heal that deep wound. I give all my guilt to You, whether false or real guilt.

Lord, help me to forget the past and look forward to what lies ahead. Thank You, Lord, for forgiving me. Now please, I ask You, fill me with such love and compassion that I can forgive those who have hurt me or who are also involved in my feeling of guilt. And help me to forgive myself.

I love You, Jesus. I praise You. I worship You. Thank You for setting me free. It's in Your name I pray. Amen.

Scriptures on Guilt

Isaiah 43:25 "I, yes, I alone am he who blots away your sins for my own sake and will never think of them again."

Psalm 32:1,2 "What happiness for those whose guilt has been forgiven! What joys when sins are covered over! What relief for those who have confessed their sins and God has cleared their record."

Romans 8:1 "So there is now no condemnation awaiting those who belong to Christ Jesus."

Ephesians 1:7 "So overflowing is his kindness towards us that he took away all our sins through the blood of his Son, by whom we are saved . . ."

Titus 3:5 ". . . then he saved us — not because we were good enough to be saved, but because of his kindness and pity — by washing away our sins and giving us the new joy of the indwelling Holy Spirit."

Hebrews 1:3 ". . . He is the one who died to cleanse us and clear our record of all sin . . ."

Hebrews 10:17 ". . . I will never again remember their sins and lawless deeds."

John 8:11 KJV ". . . Neither do I condemn thee: go, and sin no more."

Colossians 2:13-15 "You were dead in sins, and your sinful desires were not yet cut away. Then he gave you a share in the very life of Christ, for he forgave all your sins, and blotted out the charges proved against you, the list of his commandments which you had not obeyed. He took this list of sins and destroyed it by nailing it to Christ's cross. In this way God took away Satan's power to accuse you of sin, and God openly displayed to the whole world Christ's triumph at the cross where your sins were all taken away."

Romans 3:23,24 "Yes, all have sinned; all fall short of God's glorious ideal; yet now God declares us "not guilty" of offending him if we trust in Jesus Christ, who in his kindness freely takes away our sins."

Chapter Five

SET FREE FROM UNFORGIVENESS

In counseling and praying with people, we have found that so many emotional ills stem from the root cause of unforgiveness:

unforgiveness toward others,
unforgiveness toward oneself,
unforgiveness toward God.

Matthew 6:14,15 says, *"Your heavenly Father will forgive you if you forgive those who sin against you; but if you refuse to forgive them, he will not forgive you."*

Our spiritual foundation is based on forgiveness: our being forgiven by God, accepting His forgiveness, and forgiving others. I have been appalled at some of the stories we have heard as we have prayed and counseled with people. Many have been hurt so deeply, abused so badly, and treated so unfairly that sometimes I wonder, "Oh, God, how can they forgive?" But God says we must forgive.

Forgive Even a Murderer

A lady called and asked if she and her husband could come for prayer for inner healing. When they arrived, the lady shared their story. They had always been active in church. Their son had always gone to church with them until in his late teens, then he rejected their beliefs. He rejected God and said, "Mom, I don't want to go to church anymore. I want to go where there's excitement." So he joined a motorcycle gang.

In the months that followed, he tried everything Satan had to offer. He was involved in dope, sex, the occult (his girlfriend was a Satan worshiper). "Just name it," the mother said, "and he was involved in it." This did not bring him happiness, only despair and even greater restlessness. "But," she went on to say, "we never stopped praying and praising and believing God for a miracle."

Then, one day he came back home in utter misery and said, "Mom, that's not where the excitement or peace is. I'm coming back to the Lord. I want to come back home. Will you forgive me?"

"Oh," she said, "there was such jubilation and re-joicing." Then, disaster struck again. Three weeks after the son returned home, he was murdered, not by a member of the motorcycle gang, but by someone else. The man who murdered the boy was allowed to go on a probated sentence, instead of serving time in prison.

The mother said that even with this miscarriage of justice she was able to cope, and she continued to trust the Lord. "But," she said, "something happened to my husband. Our son's death began to prey on his mind, and he could not forgive the man who killed our son. His every waking thought became, 'How can I get revenge? How can I get this man behind bars?' He wrote local and federal government officials, different peace officers. He phoned one person after another, seeking recompense for our son's murder."

The wife said, "One year ago, my son died physically, but I also lost my husband spiritually. He doesn't go to church anymore. He is a broken, sad, depressed man filled with hatred and unforgiveness."

I told this couple that we believe God will heal the broken-hearted and bind up their wounds (see Psalm 147:3). We believe that He will set the captive free. I turned to the husband and said, "You have suffered a terrible loss. What this man did to your son and to you is beyond comprehension. But God wants to heal your broken heart and to set you free. There are conditions that must be met. One of the conditions is FORGIVE-NESS.

I certainly don't believe in clubbing people with scripture, and we should never heap guilt or condemnation on anyone, because at that particular moment, he is finding it hard to forgive. But I knew that unforgiveness would destroy this man. Vengeance, left unabated, would devour him. I knew it would block his entire healing.

So, I very gently reminded him that "... *Vengeance is mine, I will repay; saith the Lord" (Romans 12:19 KJV)*. I also reminded him that God's Word said, *"Whosoever hateth his brother is a murderer..." (I John 3:15 KJV)*.

We all knelt by the sofa and began to pray. My husband began by having the man renounce all the negative forces that had come against him. He named them one after another: grief, sorrow, resentment, anger, despair, depression, hopelessness, anguish, bitterness, and hatred. Then we came to the spirit of unforgiveness, and we asked him to forgive the man who had killed his son. He said, "I cannot do it."

"Would you *like* to forgive?" I asked.

I want to say here that I know it is easy for a counselor to say to a person, "Forgive." But it is another thing for a person who has been wounded so deeply to say, "Yes, I will forgive." Of course this father knew what the Bible said about forgiveness, but putting that head knowledge into his heart was something else. He said, "I just can't forgive him."

We prayed again, taking authority over the spirit of unforgiveness. Then we asked, "Would you be willing for Jesus to forgive that man through you?"

He thought for a moment and said, "Yes, I'd be willing for Jesus to forgive my son's murderer through me;" and then after a long pause, "and make me willing to forgive the man, too."

With that utterance of forgiveness, it seemed that heaven came down. We were then able to proceed and pray for the healing of all his painful memories, asking Jesus to take a spiritual eraser and heal all the deep gashes, and to anesthetize the wounds. We asked Jesus to fill the void, to fill him with peace and love, and to restore to him the joy of His salvation.

As we finished praying, Ed said to the man, "You have a physical problem, don't you? You have a short leg; isn't that right?"

"Yes, I was in an accident and suffered an injured disc, and my back has just been killing me ever since my son was killed. But how did you know that?"

Ed explained that the Lord told him so. As we prayed, the Lord realigned his back, took away the pain, and lengthened his legs to the same length. Ed said, "Now, do something you haven't been able to do before." He bent over and touched his toes.

"Why, I haven't been able to do that in years," he said. The man was absolutely amazed as he bent over again, completely free of all pain. It looked as if a veil had been lifted from his face. All the grief, unforgiveness, and bitterness had been wiped away. Joy, beautiful joy, flooded over his face.

As the couple was leaving that night, I said to the man, "You know, you have two jobs to do for the Lord: your job, and also your son's job."

He said, "You're right; I was thinking the same thing. I believe that the Lord wants me to share Jesus with that motorcycle gang. We can reach them, whereas no one else could."

Surely this is what the Lord meant when He said, *"You are to go into all the world and preach the Good News to everyone, everywhere" (Mark 16:15)* — even to motorcycle gangs.

Very few people have to go through the murder of a son as this family did, or come face to face with the giant of unforgiveness in this proportion. It's only with

the grace of our Lord that parents can overcome such a
tragic death of a loved one.

Forgiveness in Accidental Deaths

Just last week, a thirteen-year-old boy was accidentally shot to death by a seventeen-year-old boy who
supposedly was a Satan-worshiper. I talked to the
heart-broken mother right after the accident. We were
sharing that it had been just two years earlier that the
entire family (mother, husband, and sons, including this
thirteen-year-old) had been at our home for prayer for
inner healing.

The mother had so many doubts about her salvation,
but the victory over Satan had been won. The family
had grown in the Lord in such a glorious way. Then
this horrible tragedy occured. The mother said, "God
has filled me with forgiveness and she continued with
sobs in her throat, "Betty, because of our son's death,
the boy that killed him has accepted Jesus, three other
young people have accepted Jesus, and a couple on the
verge of divorce have gone back together." Even while
her mother's heart was breaking, she was forgiving the
young man who had accidentally shot and killed her
son.

The boy's funeral service was a praise service as the
minister really spoke to the eighth grade class that came
to the funeral. He shared Jesus and the plan of
salvation. He admonished these heart-broken friends and
fellow students to make their life count. He reminded
them that life is so short, we never know what will take
place the next moment; our only hope is in Jesus.

How I praise the Lord that this family is allowing Jesus to cleanse that deep, agonizing wound. How I praise Him that they have forgiven and are forgiving the boy that shot him. I thought, "You know, this must be a little of how the mother of Jesus felt as her Son was killed so that others might live. This young boy's death may have been the catalyst for bringing four people to Jesus." My prayer is that God will continue to heal the hurt that these parents have suffered and to fill the devastating loss and void with His divine love.

Not Only Forgive – But Ask Forgiveness

I was speaking at a meeting in another state when I heard a young woman share this testimony. She said that when she was five years old, her daddy left to go to work in another city. As Christmas approached, her mother said, "It isn't Christmas unless we are all together." So, she bundled all the kids up, and they went to see their daddy in the other city.

When they found the dad's apartment and got to the door, they saw him leaving with another woman. The girl continued her testimony by saying that he never came back home. They were not Christians. All the time she was growing up, when she did not have enough food to eat, the hatred would grow toward her daddy; or if she did not have enough clothes to wear, the bitterness toward her dad would grow.

Then, one day she accepted Jesus Christ. She read in the Bible that she had to forgive her daddy. When she read in Matthew 5:24, *"leave your sacrifice there beside the altar and go and apologize and be reconciled to him, and then come and offer your sacrifice to God,"* she knew that she must not only forgive her father, but she must also go and apologize and be reconciled to him. She knew she had to ask forgiveness for her attitudes of resentment, anger, bitterness, and hatred.

There are no "co-incidences" with God, just "God-incidences." Her daddy moved back to the town where she lived, and she went to see him, not only to forgive him, but to ask forgiveness from him for her bitterness, hatred, and resentment.

She said that when she knocked on the door and saw her daddy standing there, Satan brought back all the negative emotions and all the hatred. But she said, "Satan, you will not do that to me; I will forgive my dad."

Then she said, "Daddy, I just want you to know that I have accepted Jesus Christ as my Savior, and I want to ask your forgiveness for all the hatred that I have had for you all these years."

With that remark, tears started rolling down his face as he said, "Oh, but will you forgive me for all I've done to you?"

As I heard this testimony, it brought to my mind the verse in Malachi 4:6, *"His preaching will bring fathers and children together again, to be of one mind and heart . . ."* Praise You, Lord Jesus.

The Cost of Unforgiveness

Forgiving is not easy. But we cannot afford unforgiveness. The cost of unforgiveness is too high, the cost of hatred is too high, the cost of anger is too high, the cost of resentment is too high. What is the cost? Not always, but sometimes, heart problems, arthritis, or an ulcer result from unforgiveness. When there is unforgiveness we will always have inner turmoil.

A doctor and his wife came to our home for prayer. The wife was terribly crippled with arthritis. She told us, "I know I have arthritis today because I cannot forgive my husband for something he did, and because I cannot forgive myself." There had been some sins committed, and guilt was like a heavy chain around her neck.

We saw a miracle that night as the chains were broken. *"For God will break the chains that bind His people and the whip that scourges them . . ." (Isaiah 9:4).* Her hands were gnarled without any strength in them. She was unable to clench her fists. She had not been able to bend her knees; she had to walk ever so gently. After prayer for inner healing, after being set free from all guilt and unforgiveness and after prayer for healing of memories, the healing power of the Lord went through her. She was touched by the Lord — spirit, soul, and body.

When her husband came back into the room, I said, "I want you to check very carefully what the Lord has done for your wife." And with a doctor's skilled eye, he said, "Let me see you clench your hands." She did that. He said, "All right, grasp my hand," and she did so. He said, "She has not had that much strength in her hands." Then I asked her to show him what else the Lord had done for her. She sat down on the sofa and bent her legs under her, something she had not been able to do in years. Walking had been so painful, but now she began to walk around the room, lifting her feet high and placing them firmly down on the floor. Praise you, Jesus!

I was praying for a lady one night after a group inner healing meeting in Canada. She had a horrible backache. She said that it was so difficult for her to sleep at night because of the pain. I asked her how long she had experienced this, and she said, "For fourteen years." "What happened fourteen years ago?" I asked. She answered, "My child was born." Then the Lord gave that inner knowing that one of her legs was short. When we measured, one leg was about one inch shorter than the other. I started praying, asking Him to heal her back, lengthen her leg, and the leg grew out about half way, and then stopped. The Lord seemed to give another word of knowledge that she was having back problems because of unforgiveness.

I asked, "Who is it that you can't forgive?"

She said, "It was the doctor and the nurse who helped deliver my baby fourteen years ago." Even as she was saying those words it dawned on her that she had had unforgiveness all these years, and at that moment her face seemed to glow with joy. She said, "Oh, I forgive that doctor and nurse." Immediately, all the pain left her back, the legs were made the same length, and her back was healed. She stood up and twisted her back all around. She excitedly shared that for fourteen years her back had kept her from sleeping peacefully. "But tonight," she said, "I'm free from all pain. Thank You, Lord, Jesus. I'll have a good night's sleep for a change."

Dr. S. I. McMillan in *None of These Diseases* says, "The verbal expression of animosity (resentment) toward others calls forth hormones from the pituitary, adrenal, thyroid, and other glands, an excess of which can cause disease in any part of the body." He also said, "When we hate a person, we become his slave. In our own bedrooms, we cannot sleep; in our own kitchens, we cannot eat."

When we are resentful and bitter, our focus is on the offender and not on Jesus. Refusing to forgive can cause physical fatigue and lack of sleep. We may try to hide our resentments, but so often they etch themselves on our face.

Have you ever been in an office situation, and felt that your boss was a "pain in the neck," and you started having trouble with your neck or you began having headaches?

Have you gotten upset with the children at suppertime, and, disgusted with their arguing or carelessness, thought, "This makes me sick at my stomach," and you ended up with heartburn?

Doctors are the first to say that many of our ailments are caused by negative emotions. To an ulcer patient, they may ask, "What's eating you?" We may not receive our physical healing until our emotions are healed.

Resentment and unforgiveness are just like acid. Acid will eat, destroy, and corrode the container it is in before it spills out onto the shelf or floor.

Unforgiveness, if left deep inside a heart, will destroy
the person before it also spills out to harm others.
Unforgiveness eats away at your emotions.

There are fruits of unforgiveness just as there are
fruits of the Spirit:

Some of the fruits of unforgiveness toward yourself
may be: guilt, condemnation, shame, embarrassment,
unworthiness, self-hatred, and even suicide.

Some of the fruits of unforgiveness toward others
may be: hatred, bitterness, resentment, suspicion,
revenge, jealousy, and even murder.

Some of the fruits of unforgiveness toward God may
be: doubt, unbelief, and rebellion.

Forgive Unconditionally

So often we will say, "Well, I'll forgive, but I won't
forget." What we are saying is, "I'm not really forgiving." We have to forgive unconditionally; not "I'll
forgive if he stops drinking," or "I'll forgive if she
apologizes first." We have to die to self and to all our
rights. We have to say, "I have no right to self-pity. I
have no right to judge. God, You be the judge."

Our unforgiveness may block God's plan for
another's life. Bill Gothard said, "Forgiving a person is
clearing his record with us and transferring the responsibility for any punishment to God."

You may be the innocent party. But you know there
is a broken relationship. You may say to that person,
"If I've offended you, I'm sorry." You may even offer
your hand to pray, and he won't pray. You've done

your part. You are free. He is the one still in the
bondage of unforgiveness. You must turn the other
cheek and keep on loving as Christ loves. Don't spend
time worrying about what has happened in the past or
trying to get even.

Silence toward a person can be a means of trying to
punish that person. The silent person is shouting in-
wardly, "I will not forgive. I will not ask forgiveness. I
will not be reconciled."

David Augsburger wrote:

> When a betrayed trust or a fractured
> friendship stings us, we want to hold the
> grudge close, to rush to our own rescue,
> to defend ourselves to the last word, and
> to pin the blame where it is due!
>
> But forgiveness denies the self that
> demands its "rights" . . . It refuses even
> the polite little schemes we often use to
> get the other guy "back."
>
> Instead, it chooses to hurt, to suffer,
> and that is one of the hardest voluntary
> choices a man can make — to accept the
> undeserved suffering.

In 2 Corinthians 2:11, the Bible says, *"A further
reason for forgiveness is to keep from being outsmarted
by Satan; for we know what he is trying to do."* Satan
is constantly trying to put a wedge between husbands
and wives, children and parents, deacons and the pastor,
between friends, and between races.

We have even spoken in churches where there has been
a split, and we have asked what caused the problem.

Sometimes it was hard to pin-point the exact incident. How tragic that some family or church feuds may continue into the third and fourth generations, but no one remembers what caused it (see Exodus 20:5).

It's time we forgive one another. It's time we say, "I'm sorry." It's time we ask forgiveness. It's time for reconciliation. How many times are we to forgive? God's Word says in Matthew 18:21-22 that we are to forgive seventy times seven, four hundred ninety times. And we sometimes struggle over the first "I forgive," or the first "I'm sorry."

We feel "righteous indignation" when our husband or someone else hurts us. We think, "Why should I forgive? He deserves my punishment" (of silence, anger, or resentment). But whether he is right or wrong, we have to forgive. That is God's law, and we cannot break His law without consequences.

Some of the consequences of unforgiveness are poor health, negative emotions, broken relationships, broken fellowship with God, and an open door in one's life to Satan. We are really hurting ourselves when we refuse to forgive. Unforgiveness is hardly worth it.

I heard a man say one day, "Unforgiveness is like having a dead body chained to you, and you keep dragging it around behind you."

We saw a young man break those chains of unforgiveness one night. He had been in prison more than once. Before he was released the last time, his wife sent him the book, *Inner Healing Through Healing of Memories*. He read it, and when he came to the plan of salvation, he accepted Jesus Christ as his Savior. When he was released from prison, his wife called to see if he could come for prayer and counseling.

He was a huge, rough-looking man with tattoos all over his arms. The wife brought their little 18-month old baby girl with them that night.

He shared that when he was five, his mother, in a drunken stupor and rage, knocked him down some stairs, and he suffered a brain concussion. He said, "I didn't know what a normal home life was. I didn't know my father. My mother was drunk all the time. At an early age, I was out on my own. I grew up mad at the world. I was big for my age, so I fought my way through life. I was always trying to pick a fight. If anyone crossed me, I'd flatten him."

"Now I've found Jesus," he continued, "but even since I've been out of prison (six weeks), I've already struck my wife. I'm afraid of what I might do to her or my little girl. I'm still filled with rage and anger. I can't control my emotions."

We prayed the prayer of inner healing with him, taking authority over the giants of rage, anger, hatred, bitterness, violence, and sadism. When we came to the spirit of unforgiveness, he said, "Spirit of unforgiveness, out in the name of Jesus." Then, with tears in his eyes, he turned to us and said, "I've not seen my mother in fourteen years, but I'm going to write and let her know I forgive her." Oh, the healing power of Jesus is so great!

Then we prayed for healing of memories. We asked Jesus to take a spiritual eraser and wipe away every horrible memory. We prayed that the Lord would fill him with His presence, His love, joy, and peace.

When they got ready to leave that night, the daddy
picked up his little baby daughter with new tenderness.
He held her so close. I felt he was silently making a
vow, "I will never, never strike you." He hugged his
wife with new love and gentleness. We are praying that
he is walking with the Lord and being the husband and
dad the Lord meant for him to be.

Ezekiel 36:26 says, *"And I will give you a new heart
— I will give you new and right desires — and put a
new spirit within you. I will take out your stony hearts
of sin and give you new hearts of love."*

Another couple who came for prayer one night were
so angry with each other, they would barely sit together on the sofa. Even before we started the counseling session, Ed led us in prayer that God's healing power
would flow. Their divorce was to have been final in
three days. They were both Christians and did not
believe in divorce, but Satan had come against their
marriage in a horrible way and had deceived them.
They were both filled with unforgiveness. This is their
story:

The husband was a traveling salesman. He was gone
almost all the time. All the responsibility for the
children and the home was on the young wife. Even
when he was home, the husband did not know how to
show his wife that he loved her. They drifted farther
and farther apart. The flame of love grew dim, and then
died. She fell in love with someone else — a man who
showed her he loved her, who cared and was concerned,
who was responsive to her needs, who was not afraid to
show his emotions.

She went against everything she had been taught concerning adultery. She went against her high moral standards and gave in to temptation and started having an affair. All the time she knew it was wrong; she felt guilty and ashamed, but she was so starved for love; she could not say "no" to the man's advances.

When she filed for divorce, the husband realized he had failed his wife in not showing love and appreciation. He desperately started seeking help through prayer and counseling.

I asked the husband, "Do you still love your wife?"

"Oh, yes, very much, and I know I have failed her, but I want another chance."

I turned to the wife and asked the same question. "Do you love your husband?"

She very bluntly, but honestly said, "No, I don't. I love this other man."

"Did you love your husband when you married him?"

"Yes, I did," she answered.

"Would you like to love him again?"

She thought for a moment, weighing the question. Then she said, "I know divorce would hurt our children so much. I know we are Christians and the Bible says we should not divorce. And I know we ought to be able to work this out if we can." Then she paused for a long time, really searching her heart. "Yes," she said, "I suppose I would like to love him again."

But even as she said these words, there was still bitterness and unforgiveness in her voice.

I shot a prayer silently to God and said, "Oh, dear Lord, please do a miracle."

Ed prayed for the husband, and I prayed for the wife in separate rooms. We each asked the Lord to set them free from all the negative emotions and to heal the hurts and painful memories. We took authority over all the giants that had come against them. In the name of Jesus we bound the giants of unforgiveness, bitterness, hate, rejection, resentment.

We prayed that the Lord would wipe away all the painful memories. Then we prayed for them together as a couple that the Lord would strengthen and bless their marriage. This couple has moved away, but the last time we heard from them, the husband wrote to say, "Our marriage has never been better. We have forgiven each other. We are active in church ... We praise the Lord for the miracle He performed in our lives that night."

I don't want to give the impression that all the sessions have ended as successfully as this one, or that all sessions have ended with an immediate miracle, because they have not!

God will do His part, but we each have to do our part, also. This couple was willing to work at salvaging their marriage. God honored their prayers and desires, and the marriage was healed. This all happened because they were willing to *forgive* and be *forgiven.*

Teaching Our Children to Forgive

We must teach our children to forgive. A child learns to forgive by watching his parents forgive and ask forgiveness. When we as parents are wrong, we need to go to our child and say, "Son, I was wrong. Will you forgive me?"

When our children are just tiny tots (two and three), it isn't too early to start laying the foundation of forgiveness. When a neighbor child breaks a toy, say to your son or daughter, "I know that was your favorite toy, but I'm sure your friend did not mean to break it. Let's forgive him, shall we?"

If a child learns at a young age to say "I forgive," then he won't have as many problems forgiving when the deep hurts come later in life. Many marriages end in divorce because neither partner learned to say, "I forgive you," or, "I'm sorry." Mrs. Billy Graham was quoted as saying, "The secret of a happy marriage is two good forgivers."

If there has been a divorce, the rejection, loneliness, and hurt that come against the child is bad enough without letting the wound become infected with the poison of hatred and unforgiveness. As difficult as it may be, try to teach your child to forgive the parent who caused the divorce. If hatred is allowed to stay, the child may grow up to be an emotional cripple.

Parents, when a child breaks a household rule or literally breaks your most cherished possession, forgive that child and don't hold it over his head continually. Forgive and forget.

Larry Christianson in *The Christian Family* says,
After a child has been spanked, the father should kneel down with him and have the child ask God's forgiveness for the specific sin committed. ("Dear God,

please forgive me for sassing Mommy.")
The father may then want to pray also,
thanking God for the forgiveness which
He gives through the blood of Christ. If
we take seriously the father's priestly
role in the family, it would not be at all
out of place then to lay your hand upon
the child and declare to him the forgiveness which God has given through
Christ. And then your own forgiveness
should also be expressed — most effec-
tively with a hug and a kiss. For this is
the goal of all discipline: forgiveness and
reconciliation.

Children many times feel unforgiveness toward
coaches, teachers, neighbors, certain races of people, or
churches. They really don't know why they feel the
way they do. They are just mimicking their parents'
own negative attitudes of unforgiveness, resentment and
prejudice.

When a child is treated unfairly or punished un-
wisely, we as parents should listen sympathetically and
lovingly. We should let the child know how sorry we
are, and how our heart aches for him. Then, after the
child has been able to pour out his or her hurt, a wise
parent will say, "Now, let's both forgive that person
who has hurt you, and let's pray for him." Pray also
that God will heal your child's hurt feelings.

There are times we may even have to forgive an
animal. We received a letter from a girl in Canada that
said she had to forgive a dog. Here is her letter:

Dear Betty,

After attending an inner healing service conducted by you and your husband, I was led to read your book. Through these two blessed vehicles of God, a most wonderful healing has taken place deep in my heart.

When I was five years old, a neighbor and his dog came to visit our farm. While there, his dog killed my "kitty" who had been my closest companion for as long as I could remember. From my living room window, I watched my white Persian kitty suffer and die out on the snow. I said to myself, "I'm a big girl, and big girls don't cry." I stifled my tears and buried a pain that tore me apart. Subsequently I forgot about it.

Twenty-six years later, after reading your book, the Holy Spirit revealed this incident to me, and I wept as I've never done before. I knew the Lord asks us to forgive others, but I never thought He would ask me to forgive a dog.

As I retraced the steps of this painful, but buried memory, I saw Jesus walk over to my "kitty." He picked up her lifeless form and came toward me. As He stood before me, He restored her broken body, gave her life again, and said, "She is such a beautiful kitty. May I keep her until you come to stay with Me?"

Thank you for being an obedient
servant of the Lord in bringing His wonderful message of inner healing to His
people. There is a new peace within me.

THREE AREAS OF FORGIVENESS

Remember, before inner healing takes place, there
must be three types of forgiveness:
1. We must accept God's forgiveness of our sins.
2. We must forgive others.
3. We must forgive ourselves.

Accept God's Forgiveness

*I John 1:9 "But if we confess our sins to him, he
can be depended on to forgive us and to cleanse us
from every wrong..."*
*II Corinthians 5:20-21 "... we beg you, as though
Christ himself were here pleading with you, receive the
love he offers you — be reconciled to God. For God
took the sinless Christ and poured into him our sins.
Then, in exchange, he poured God's goodness into us!"*
Have you asked forgiveness for your sins? Have you
confessed your sins to God? The basic foundation of all
healing comes through forgiveness. If you're not sure
about salvation, if you have doubts, if you don't know
that you know that all your sins are forgiven and that
Jesus is your Savior, would you take the following
steps:
1.   Confess your sins and ask forgiveness from Jesus.

2. Forgive those who have sinned against you.
3. Invite Jesus into your heart as your personal Savior.
4. Turn your back on sin and ask Jesus to take control of your life.

Would you say the following prayer. Even though you've said this prayer before, repeat it again. God does not want you to have doubts about your salvation. He does not want you to doubt that you've been forgiven. Please know that if you're truly repentant, God is faithful and just to forgive you.

PRAYER FOR SALVATION

(Accepting God's Forgiveness)

Lord Jesus, I know I am a sinner and have sinned. I confess my sins to You. I ask forgiveness of all my sins — those sins I remember and those sins I've forgotten about. I forgive those who have sinned against me.

Lord Jesus, come into my heart as my Savior. I surrender my life to You. I make You Lord of my heart and life. I commit myself totally and completely to You. Thank You for coming into my heart as my personal Savior. I love You and want to serve You forever. Amen.

I want you to write the date in your Bible when you committed your life to Christ. Then, when Satan comes against you with doubts, you can say, "Satan, you are a liar and a deceiver. On this date written in my Bible, I asked forgiveness of my sins. I asked Jesus into my heart, and He is in my heart as Lord of my life."

Because we are human, we will sin again and again. We should never try to hide our sins and bad attitudes from the Lord. He knows all about them. One of the things that made David a "man after God's own heart" was the fact that David honestly confessed his sin to God. He sinned, terribly, but he was deeply convicted of his sin. He had a broken spirit. He was filled with remorse and penitence, and he came before the Lord with a contrite heart (Psalm 51).

We must do the same. God is not interested in our flippant, half-hearted response of "I'm sorry," but He is interested in our deep repentance as we come before Him and ask His forgiveness.

God forgave David, and He likewise will forgive us. David did have to live with some of the consequences of his sin, and we may have to face that penalty also. But we are forgiven, and God remembers our sins no more.

Forgive Others

Matthew 5:24 ". . . leave your sacrifice there beside the altar and go apologize and be reconciled to him . . ."

Matthew 6:14-15 "Your heavenly Father will forgive you if you forgive those who sin against you; but if you refuse to forgive them, he will not forgive you."

Colossians 3:13 "Be gentle and ready to forgive; never hold grudges. Remember, the Lord forgave you, so you must forgive others."

Catherine Marshall in her book, *Something More*, has a chapter on forgiveness entitled, "The Aughts and the Anys." In this chapter, she wrote that each person should make a list of all the grievances he has against others (husband, children, friends). Then, pray the prayer of relinquishment and lift these people to the Lord and forgive them of each offense, no matter how small or trivial.

It is especially imperative to forgive those in our family. We are sometimes negligent in saying, "I'm sorry," to those closest to us. We are also sometimes slow about saying, "I forgive you." And in any family there will be times when "I'm sorry," or, "I forgive you," need to be exchanged — and quickly.

Let me caution you. Don't ever ask forgiveness of someone if that person has not been aware of your feelings. Your confession of resentment or unforgiveness (if he has not been aware of your feelings) would only make a wound where there had been no wound before.

If the person is not aware of your feelings, then you make your confession to the Lord. If, however, each person knows there is a broken relationship, if there have been words spoken in anger, then ask forgiveness and try to be reconciled.

If you have spread gossip or spoken behind someone's back, go to the person you have talked about, confess what you have done, and ask forgiveness. Then try to make things right with the people to whom you have spoken.

Some people have to forgive an entire denomination. A precious Catholic lady was so embittered toward a nun who had taught her and had been unkind to her and toward a priest, that she had to forgive her entire church. After we finished praying, she said, "I need to forgive the Pope for some of his stands on doctrine," and that's exactly what she did. Then she asked God's forgiveness for her own bad attitudes.

I don't share this story to single out any particular church, for this was an exception to the general rule. Some of our dearest friends are Catholic nuns and priests. We have shared in many Catholic groups, and have seen the love that they have for Jesus. Their love for Him just glows on their faces. You may have unforgiveness toward your own pastor, rector, Sunday School teacher, or denomination. Please forgive them and pray for them.

A German lady who was in a neutral country during the second World War was persecuted and ostracized as a child. She grew up with a deep feeling of unforgiveness and feelings of fear and rejection. She realized that she had to forgive an entire race of people and the entire country who had persecuted her. After forgiveness and a prayer for inner healing, she seemed to stand straighter. A weight had been lifted from her shoulders. She seemed to hold her head just a little bit higher.

Would you ask the Lord to reveal to you if there are those whom you need to forgive. Make a list of all the offenses that you need to forgive, as well as the offenders.

"And when ye stand praying, forgive, if ye have aught against any: that your Father also which is in heaven may forgive you your trespasses (Mark 11:25 KJV).

Perhaps this list will help you:

husband or wife	teachers
children	principals
parents or stepparents	church or pastors
in-laws	employer or employees
grandparents	a certain race of people
aunts, uncles, cousins	a country or government
former mate	friends
the "other" person	neighbors
inanimate object	doctors or nurses
policemen	an animal

And even though we don't like to think about it, have you ever had unforgiveness toward God? Have you blamed Him for something? Do you need to say, "God, I forgive You"? And then ask forgiveness for your own bitterness or resentment.

After you have made your list, go through the entire list and forgive each person for each offense. Each day practice "spiritual housecleaning." Immediately, constantly, continually forgive those who hurt you. Not only forgive them, but pray for them.

PRAYER TO FORGIVE OTHERS

Lord, I lift up the following people to You. (Name them, each one.) I confess I've had unforgiveness, but I want to be

set free. I want to forgive. Satan, you
are bound from me in the name of
Jesus. Spirits of unforgiveness, rage,
hatred, bitterness, resentment, revenge,
and retaliation, you are bound from me
in the name of Jesus.
  I forgive each person (dead or alive)
who has hurt me. I ask, Lord, that You
would wipe the memory of the incident
from my mind. Cleanse the wound, set
me free, break the chains, and fill me
with Your forgiveness. Lord Jesus, I
want to pray for those who have hurt
me, and Lord, please help me to truly
mean it. Fill me with Your love, and a
spirit of forgiveness. In Jesus' name I
pray. Amen.

  After you have forgiven someone, then do something
constructive: write a letter, make a visit, telephone
them, buy a joy gift, or send a card. If Jesus could say
as He was being nailed to the cross, "Father, forgive,"
surely we can take the step after we forgive, to do
something concrete to build a bridge of forgiveness with
kindness.
  David Augsburger in *The Freedom of Forgiveness*
says:
    "(Forgiveness) gives love where the
    enemy expected hatred. It gives freedom
    where the enemy deserves punishment. It
    gives understanding where the enemy
    anticipated revenge."

Forgive Yourself

Romans 8:1 "So there is now no condemnation awaiting those who belong to Christ Jesus."
John 8:11 KJV "... Neither do I condemn thee: go, and sin no more."

It is so imperative that we accept God's forgiveness and forgive ourselves. We cannot be totally healed or set free until we can forgive our mistakes.

Going to a pastor, priest, or counselor and confessing a sin and hearing that person say, "God forgives you," will often enable you to forgive yourself.

Be very careful, however, about sharing your feelings of guilt with just any acquaintance. Only if you have a friend who is a tried and tested mature Christian, should you confess your intimate, personal indiscretions or negative emotions. We have prayed and counseled with some people who had been hurt even more when their confessions to a friend (shared in privacy) were later shared with the entire prayer group or had "leaked out" to the entire church.

Not forgiving ourselves is actually a form of rebellion. We are in truth saying to God, "I don't believe Your Word that says You won't remember my sins." We are saying to God, "I am going to judge myself. I will not accept Your judgment and verdict of 'not guilty.' In fact, I have judged myself, and I have found myself guilty and unpardonable."

Do you suppose we are sinning when we do not forgive ourselves? This very act separates us from God. God's Word says we must forgive — that means even ourselves.

A middle-aged lady who came for prayer could not
forgive herself. She was so bowed down with guilt and
condemnation. With tears in her eyes, she said, "I'm the
worst person on this earth. Nobody is worse than I
am."

Her feelings of guilt were the root cause of emotional, physical, and spiritual problems. She could not
or would not forgive herself.

She married at fourteen, had a baby at fifteen, one
at sixteen, and another at seventeen. The third child
died when it was three months old. Then she became
pregnant again. After the fourth child at age eighteen,
she went into a deep depression. She also had many
physical problems. The doctor said, "You absolutely
must not have any more children," even though she was
in a denomination that did not condone birth control.

Because of the seriousness of her condition, when she
became pregnant for the fifth time in that many years,
her medical doctor said, "To save your life, I must
perform an abortion." She talked to her priest about
the problems, and he said, "I cannot give you permission, but I will forgive you if you have the abortion
performed." So she had the abortion, but she felt so
terribly guilty.

Then she became pregnant with number six, and
again, the doctor said, "You may not live if you have
any more children." When she became pregnant again,
he performed another abortion. She was so miserable,
depressed, physically sick, unhappy with her marriage,
and so overcome with guilt. She divorced the husband
who wanted her to keep on having the yearly babies,
and later she remarried.

There were other sins committed during the years
that also made her unable to accept God's forgiveness
or to forgive herself. She was sick — spirit, soul, and
body, all because she was so bowed down with guilt and
condemnation, and because she was unable to forgive
herself.

We prayed with her for inner healing, taking authority over that spirit of unforgiveness toward herself and
the spirits of self-hatred, guilt, condemnation, and so
on. We asked the Lord to fill her with His love to such
a point that she could forgive herself. The power of the
Lord came over her, and we could see the healing
power of Jesus sweep through her body.

God even did spiritual surgery that day. He actually
healed her hiatal hernia right before our eyes.

She had always felt that she had no right to God's
happiness and peace because of her guilt. Satan had
deceived her with his lies. But praise God, the joy of
the Lord was so evident on her face that day as she
forgave herself and felt God's healing power flow
through her.

If you are having trouble forgiving yourself, keep
reminding yourself that God's Word says you are forgiven. And as the little song goes, "If the Lord says I
am, then I am."

God is saying to you that He loves you, that He has
forgiven all your sins, and He wants you to forgive
yourself. Don't be your own judge. God is the One who
judges. When you confess your sins, the slate is cleaned.
YOU ARE FORGIVEN. God doesn't remember what
you are talking about when you go over your past
confessed sins. NOW FORGIVE YOURSELF.

PRAYER TO FORGIVE YOURSELF

Thank You, Lord, for Your Word that
says if I confess my sins, You will
remember them no more, that You will
send them into the deepest oceans. Lord
Jesus, please help me forgive myself.
Help me to forgive myself for the accident I caused, or the mistake I made,
the gossip I shared, all the things I
should have done, but didn't do and all
the things I did but shouldn't have. Help
me to forgive myself for wrong choices
either in marriage or in my profession.
Lord Jesus, please help me not to judge
myself, but to accept Your forgiveness
and to forgive myself. In Your name I
pray. Amen.

There is an old, old saying, "Put Jesus first, others
second, and yourself last, and then you will have joy. I
want to add to that and say,
  J   — Jesus — Accept Jesus' forgiveness, first
  O   — Others — Forgive others who have hurt you,
         second
  Y   — Yourself — Forgive yourself third.
  When you do those three things, you will have the
joy that only God can give. Bless you.

David Augsburger, in his book *The Freedom of
Forgiveness,* wrote some beautiful truths concerning

forgiveness. With his permission, I want to quote them
for you:

> Doing an injury puts you below your
> enemy; revenging an injury makes you
> but even with him; forgiving it sets you
> above him!

> Forgetting is the result of complete for-
> giveness; it is never the means. It is the
> final step, not the first.

> If you hold back forgiveness until the
> offender deserves it, forget it! That's not
> forgiveness! Forgive immediately!
> Forgive when the first hurt is
> felt! . . . forgive before the sting has
> begun to swell.

> The grease of forgiving love can reduce
> the friction and salve the irritation.

> Forgetful forgiveness is not a case of
> holy amnesia which erases the past. No,
> instead it is the experience of healing
> which draws the poison from the wound.

> (Forgiveness) brings new life to our
> withered hearts, new energy to our
> paralyzed emotions, new understanding
> to our frozen feelings.

SCRIPTURES ON FORGIVENESS

Colossians 3:13 "Be gentle and ready to forgive; never hold grudges. Remember, the Lord forgave you, so you must forgive others."

Matthew 6:14,15 "Your heavenly Father will forgive you if you forgive those who sin against you; but if you refuse to forgive them, he will not forgive you."

Ephesians 4:32 "Instead, be kind to each other, tenderhearted, forgiving one another, just as God has forgiven you because you belong to Christ."

Matthew 18:21,22 "Then Peter came to him and asked, 'Sir, how often should I forgive a brother who sins against me? Seven times?'
'No!' Jesus replied, 'seventy times seven!' "

Mark 11:25-26 KJV. "And when you stand praying, forgive if ye have aught against any: that your Father, also which is in heaven may forgive you your trespasses. But if ye do not forgive, neither will your Father which is in heaven forgive your trespasses."

Chapter Six

SET FREE TO SERVE

The salvation experience of inviting Jesus into our hearts is not the end — it is only the glorious beginning of our walk with the Lord. The in-filling of the Holy Spirit is not the end; it is only the beginning when we receive the power to do the job the Lord has for us to do. It is not a one time experience but a daily being filled with the Spirit.

There are many who say, "I'm filled with the Spirit," but others don't see the fruit of the Spirit in their lives. By the fruit of the Spirit we are known. We can be Christians, even Spirit-filled Christians, but not be free to live the vibrant, productive life God had planned for us.

The following testimonies are of ladies who are intelligent and talented, but it was only when they had a special touch from Jesus, it was only when they allowed Him to set them free from hindering forces, that they were able to live up to their magnificent potential. Some were bowed down with the chains of fear, guilt, rejection, grief, depression, inferiority, nightmares, and pain; but Jesus broke the chains.

They had been in the cocoons of bondage, but when Jesus touched them, they were free — free to be the Spirit-filled Christians He wanted them to be. The Lord doesn't heal us just for ourselves. He heals us and sets us free to serve and to lead others to Him. These stories are shared for one reason only — TO LIFT JESUS UP! We give all the praise and glory to Him.

Set Free From Rejection and Guilt

Dear Betty,

Please use my testimony as you choose. I came from a home of two unequally yoked parents who had four unwanted children. I was molested by a relative and raped by a neighbor. This was totally degrading and a humiliation to me. I was constantly told by my parents that I was no good and would never be anything. My parents said that they couldn't wait until I married.

I knew rejection to the ultimate. I was seldom ever touched until I began to date. I craved attention. In school I cheated and failed. I even became a kleptomaniac and was arrested twice.

I entered into a marriage relationship determined to make it work. But with all my effort, I became more frustrated and exhausted. It seemed the harder I tried, the worse it became. I felt rejection from my husband because he was always hunting and fishing. I committed adultery with anyone who asked · usually my boss. I never drank; I did all this totally sober.

After years of this horrible way of living and several children !ater, I felt I couldn't cope with life anymore. I wanted to die. I always wore a smiling mask, but on the inside, I was miserable and was filled with inner turmoil. I ate everything in sight trying to satisfy my inner longing for happiness.

Even though I was a church member and even had been active in church, I had no joy. I began searching for God to make Himself real to me, and He did. He filled me with His Holy Spirit. He gave me a "hot-line" to heaven and immersed me in His love. He flooded my soul with joy.

But by now, I tipped the scales at 200 pounds and wore a dress size 24½. I knew Jesus wanted to be Lord of all, or He wasn't Lord at all. I knew I couldn't lose weight alone. I tried with all my heart to lose weight, but I couldn't. I had wounds from my past that haunted me. Memories that I couldn't erase seemed to control my behavior. And yet, I desired that the Holy Spirit hold the reins of my life.

It was at this time that I heard of the Tapscotts' Inner Healing Ministry. I knew that I was a prime candidate. When I attended their meeting, I walked back through my past hand-in-hand with Jesus. He used His spiritual eraser and removed from my memory my fears and frustrations. He gave me love for hate, and peace for turmoil. I was set free from resentment and bitterness that had controlled me for years. I was as free as a bird.

His shed blood has cleansed me from all my sins. He removed all my guilt. I've experienced the reality of Jesus. I'm a living proof that when the Son sets you free, you are free indeed. God made something beautiful out of my life. When I received inner healing, I was able to receive my physical healing. I now weigh 130 pounds and wear a size 9-10 dress. To God be the glory for the things He has done.

Now, my one goal is to serve Jesus and be a witness for Him.

Love,

Set Free From Fear and Nightmares and Inferiority

I grew up as a Catholic although not a devout one
due to all my home problems. Through another church,
I accepted Christ; I was the only Christian in my
family. My parents divorced, and my mother was left
with virtually nothing. She became very despondent in
trying to help us just survive. She finally became
physically and emotionally unable to cope. I kept
turning to church and school to better myself.

Our home was not only poor, but also unkempt. I
was terrified of the rats that were always there. I even
had dreams of the rats. My mother would be gone for
days and nights at a time. Finally out of desperation
and fear of being alone with the ever-present rats, I left
home.

I was able, by God's goodness, to attend a Bible
school. But I found it so difficult to relate to my peers
because of my bad self-image and inferiority complex. I
was defensive and hostile to my friends and to authority. I assumed a pseudo-superiority mask as a cover-up.
I often questioned the professors and took the defensive when there wasn't anything to defend.

I so desperately wanted to make something of myself.
I was thrilled when after graduation, I was given the job
as the Director of Christian Education of a large church.
This was my dream come true. But again, my past
feelings of inferiority came back, and I found myself
always defensive and antagonistic. I always felt that
because I was a woman, I was being discriminated
against.

About this time, a worker in my church had an experience with the Holy Spirit and was literally a new person. My inner-most thoughts were, "Do you suppose there's hope for me, too?" I went to her home and questioned her about what had happened. She suggested that I have prayer for inner healing. So I contacted Betty Tapscott and made an appointment.

Praise the Lord! After prayer for healing of memories, I was transformed. It's hard to describe how anyone can be a domineering women's libber, analytical and intellectual-sounding one day, and the very next day feel gentleness and a willingness to follow the leading of the Holy Spirit.

Shortly after my inner healing, my husband and I moved to another state where I became the principal of a church school and my husband was the associate minister. My husband was amazed at my newly found confidence. I give all the glory to Jesus. My job as principal was a success — in the inter-personal relationships with my teachers, and with the financial side of running a school. We were also able to uphold the highest Christian principles.

My husband and I realize that God is our Source. In ourselves, we can do nothing. How wonderful it is to reach out to help others.

Set Free From Grief, Depression and Headaches

I desired to be a victorious Christian. I had done many good works in my fundamental church, but when it seemed impossible to live up to the "holiness" standards of my church, I drifted away from God. My husband and I became nominal Christians. Things of the world seemed more important.

When one of our four children developed cancer at the age of ten, it seemed that our world caved in. Day after day, the pain and frustration of watching our son die put my husband and me into a state of bitterness and depression. I suffered migraine headaches and became unable to hold a job.

After our son's death, I withdrew into a world of sickness and despair. I even got to the point of doubting my salvation. I knew my son was in heaven, but I was afraid I would never see him there. I gave up all hope. I just knew I was going to Hell.

Friends prayed and counseled with me, and I regained a measure of hope. I took a good job, but once again, my physical health failed, and I couldn't maintain the position. I had absolutely no self-confidence at all.

Someone referred me to Betty Tapscott, and I went for inner healing. I've never been the same since. Praise the Lord! I've never had another migraine headache. God healed me physically and emotionally. He filled me with boldness and confidence.

A short time later, I was appointed the administrator of our Accelerated Christian Education school. I have had tremendous success in this position, thanks to Jesus. My friends say my countenance radiates Jesus. And I do feel joy — wonderful joy.

I want to be a living witness of Jesus' changing power to everyone I come in contact with. I know exactly where I will spend eternity — it's with my Lord and my little son who awaits me. I praise Him for setting me free from grief and depression and for helping me to be able to use the administrative talents he gave me.

Serve Where You Are

I had been in a fundamental, Bible-believing church for about twenty-five years. We were taught salvation and the infilling of the Holy Spirit, but we were not taught how to maintain this victorious life. I really tried very hard, year after year, to live up to our church's standards. I was an excellent employee of the church, and this was so successful, that somehow, I managed to keep at least a "working" experience with the Lord. God graciously blessed me with my family, public school—teaching profession, and my church work.

So I was successful, but not victorious. I was happy, but not joyful. The one thing missing was a personal, spiritual relationship with Jesus. I began to give up the hope of ever having one. As a matter of fact, I came to the point of unbelief. I decided to keep on doing my church work, but I just wouldn't seek the Lord anymore. He was not there, I decided, and the devil was just an evil force.

About that same time, God sovereignly reached down and touched my life. Through a completely unexpected move from what we thought was our permanent home and school situation, we found ourselves in a new school district. In my new school, my daughter was placed in the room of a Spirit-filled teacher. I soon noticed that of all the Christians I had known, this one was different. Joy radiated from her.

I asked her what caused her to have such joy and peace. She quickly said, "Oh, it's the Holy Spirit." So I

started reading books on the Spirit-filled life. I asked
questions and read the Bible in a new way — seeking
answers.

Then, one day, I again repeated the sinner's prayer. I
asked Jesus to come into my heart. I asked Him to fill
me with His Holy Spirit — and He did — to overflowing.

My life was transformed. I couldn't get enough
worship. I couldn't quench my thirst by reading the
Bible enough.

Soon after this experience, I was in a book store one
day. I saw the book, *Inner Healing Through Healing of
Memories,* and a tape on the subject. I knew from the
traumatic episodes in early childhood that I needed
inner healing. My parents divorced when I was three.
My mother married someone else, divorced him, and
remarried my father.

I was married to a successful school counselor, but
we had problems at home also. One of the problems
involved our beautiful, successful son who had a
psycho-motor problem surface at age nine. This resulted
in a dramatic behavioral change and some noticeable
retardation in learning and maturation.

Anyway, I bought the book and the tape. I filled out
a card asking for an appointment with Betty. This even
changed my life more. Several weeks later, when it was
time for my appointment, I went over, shaking in my
boots.

Shortly after I got there, while we were just sharing,
a feeling sort of like choking or something being
crowded into my throat and chest came over me. I

showed no manifestation of this, but felt panicky as I had never before experienced it.

I saw Betty begin to pray silently in the Spirit, and it went away. Later, I found out that she felt the same sensation. We prayed the prayer of inner healing, and I was completely overpowered by the Lord.

I left that day feeling that a whole mountain was lifted from me. I was, at the time, being considered for a principal or assistant's job, and I thought my life depended on it. Betty told me that the Lord had my life charted out, and that He had a perfect plan for me. He would work out my profession. So I decided to let Him do it. The Lord gave her a prophecy that people would begin to come to me for ministry at school, and that sounded far out. But at this point, I just wanted to do what the Lord said.

So I went on my way and started living the most glorious life I had ever known. I began to discover that inner healing works and works and keeps on working. A week and a month later, I kept discovering areas that were healed. I'm still discovering them!

Perhaps the most immediate healing was that of headaches. I often had "regular" ones, but on occasion, I would have a real headache that went on for 24 to 48 hours. When I was saturated with pain medicine, I would finally get desperate and go to the emergency room for a real knock-out shot. I have never had a bad headache since praying with Betty. I have stopped my pain prescription. If I once in a while have a little headache, it soon goes away.

Meanwhile, at school, people began to notice a dramatic change in me. Sure enough, they began to

come for ministry. Slowly, my desire to become a
school administrator went away, and the Lord sort of
gave me a beautiful gift for being obedient to His plan.
*I was nominated for Teacher of the Year, which "I"
won. To top it off, I received Second Runner-Up in the
Texas State Competition.*

A book compiling my accomplishments included
many religious articles that I had written that had been
published. These lifted up Jesus and were read very
widely. In addition, newspapers and reporters printed
what I said about my help from God in the classroom,
and this witnessed to thousands more.

It just seems that the Holy Spirit is in control as I
teach public school, teach my adult Sunday School
class, and serve as our church's only woman lay-
minister. I regularly counsel at the 700 Club, leading
people into the infilling of the Holy spirit. Miracles of
healing and all sorts of miracles are happening all the
time. Only the Lord could do this, and I give Him all
the credit. God is continually opening up new avenues
of writing as well as the witnessing through public
speaking and counseling.

Lastly, my school teaching includes miracles that
stagger the natural mind. God can teach anything. He
can even heal little broken hearts and touch hyperactive
children. As I allow Him to speak His power to any
problem, He is able and willing to handle it. We also
have a far-reaching teachers disciple group, and we're
learning "How To Release the Power of the Holy Spirit
In The Classroom." I guess this is the shortest story I've
ever written, because to tell it all would take a book.
Praise the Lord.

Set Free — Indeed

The previous testimony was written by an outstanding teacher in the sixth largest city in the United States. She just recently was elected Teacher of the Year in a school district that is noted nationally for its outstanding schools. The year she was elected Teacher of the Year, 9,500 applicants applied for the 100 vacant teaching positions in this district. She was also the second runner up in the state of Texas Teacher of the Year Competition.

Her point of contact for serving the Lord is in her public school classroom. Teaching, showing love and gentleness, inspiring, admonishing, being a friend to the fellow teachers as well as students is how she shares Jesus where she is. She has given back to the Lord her many talents of music, writing poetry, and writing articles for professional education, and church magazines. He is blessing her endeavors in such a beautiful way.

She is one who will whole-heartedly agree that in Him we can do all things. On her classroom door she has the sign, "You are a promise." Her testimony along with the others in this chapter is one of praise to God for being SET FREE. May God set you free also to be the person He created you to be. May He fill you with the Holy Spirit, and the fruit of the Spirit. May you be SET FREE to do the job the Lord has for you to do.

REMEMBER

You are loved, You are special and —
"... *if the Son sets you free, you will indeed be free.*"

John 8:36

Books written by BETTY TAPSCOTT

INNER HEALING THROUGH HEALING OF MEMORIES
THE FRUIT OF THE SPIRIT
OUT OF THE VALLEY
SET FREE
SELF-IMAGE*
PERDONAR Y SANIDAD INTERIOR (Spanish)*
FORGIVENESS AND INNER HEALING*
*Co-Author Father Robert DeGrandis

Available at your favorite bookstore

or

Order copies from
Betty Tapscott
Box 19827
Houston, Texas 77224

Pamphlet: Inner Healing   4 / $1.00
                       (Large Print)   2 / $1.00
      Available in English or Spanish (Quantity Discounts)

CASSETTE TAPES: $4.00 each
Teaching Tape on Inner Healing
Testimony and Ministering Inner Healing
SET FREE Series   (Send for complete list.)

Prices Subject to change

1-2 books $1.00 postage and handling
3-4 books $1.25 postage and handling
5-books $1.50 postage and handling